ON BEING A KID IN THE 1940s
A MEMOIR

ON BEING A KID IN THE 1940s
A MEMOIR

THOMAS F. LEE

This book is dedicated to my parents, Mary Blanchard Lee and Bernard Thomas Lee

It is difficult for a man to speak long of himself without vanity, therefore I shall be short.
David Hume, 1776

INTRODUCTION

I am going into the past, back to Hendy's. That is not the official name of that small pond lying just over the hill from my Worcester home. It's just what my friends and I called that magical, shallow basin of water, no bigger than half a football field. It formed where the slender stream meandering through a nearby cow pasture ended, and the flow briefly paused before it found a new course, and ran down an incline into the woods.

It has always been easy to get there. All I need to do is to go back in time. I get out of bed, put on a pair of corduroys, a short-sleeved shirt, and my high top sneakers. Then, a quick breakfast of oatmeal with my two grandmothers, and a brief stop in the back porch to pick up my yellow fiberglass rod with a casting reel full of ten lb. test line (tough enough to handle a really big fish) and my box of lures. I might decide to grab my battered wicker creel and put a can of night crawlers in there, along with a red and white bobber and a few lead sinkers.

Then, out the back door, down the short path to the sidewalk, and a quick run across the street. After clambering up a steep embankment, aided by stepping on the handy root of a massive oak tree, I can begin the short trek up through the tall, golden grass of Hendy's field.

When I get to the crest of the hill, I can see the faint path leading down to the scene below – the pond, now

1

about five hundred yards away, the broad green cow pasture behind that, and to my right, the woods, a mix of oaks, maples and birches.

The morning sun is warm on my back as I head down the path full of anticipation. That pond is full of pickerel, perch, horned pout, and even suckers that breed up in the creek. There are huge bullfrogs waiting, their bulbous heads jutting out from the shallows. If you put a piece of red cloth on a hook and dangle it in front of one of them, it will jump and grab that temptation. Then you will have yourself a nice frog to examine and throw back.

Good thing I have my slingshot with me in my back pocket. There will be plenty of stuff to shoot at like those same frogs, or a bird in the bushes, or maybe a squirrel or two. And what is there to worry about? Not a thing. I'm eleven years old and school is over for the year. It's time to just have fun.

* * *

I did go back to Hendy's 70 years later. I drove down to Worcester from New Hampshire, and found my way back to the old neighborhood. As I drove past my former house, still sitting there on the corner of Main and Eureka Streets, although now in the form of a hairdressing salon, I was suddenly disoriented.

Where Hendy's field once lay, open to the sunshine, were rows of houses. How could a kid get up to the pond through those yards and driveways? I kept on driving to the corner of Apricot Street and took a right, knowing that I could easily swing up onto Wildwood Ave and drive right past the farmer's house. From there, I could get a good view of the pond from the road. Maybe there would be a couple of kids fishing.

But the pond was nowhere to be seen. Instead, there were more houses, and a road that seemed to be running straight into the woods. I knew where the pond must be, somewhere down in the hollow that I assumed must be there behind those houses, because I could see the tops of trees growing down where the cow pasture used to be.

I knew that the pond must be there. I mean, how can you remove a pond and a stream? The water just keeps on coming, doesn't it? And where is a kid supposed to fish and catch frogs?

(Note: At this writing, I discover that Hendy's appears on both Google and Apple maps – unlabeled and of different, inaccurate shapes.)

* * *

I don't want to go back again and try to work my way down through the underbrush to what may be left of Hendy's Pond. Not because I am afraid of what I might see, but because even if not a trace remains of that magical site, it remains as real to me as my own self. The golden field, the narrow path, the pond filled with anticipated possibilities – these all live in my memory, and I have experienced those treasured moments in my mind time and time again over the years.

When adolescence arrives, and high school years begin, a door closes imperceptibly. It cannot be opened again from the far side. Being a kid is not just a physical state. More importantly, it is a state of mind in which wonder and mystery reign. Back then, my world consisted of family, friends, church, and school, coexisting comfortably within a few blocks, while the rest of the world inhabited the far edges, not yet in focus.

Over the last few years, as I approached and then attained the age of 80, I often thought about writing an account of what life was like when I was a kid – in my case, between the years 1938 to 1950.

I never intended my story to be a strict historical record, as in a sociologist's or historian's account of those times, now disappearing rapidly in the rearview mirror. Those records exist in abundance. Instead, I began to realize, as I started to gather together the images and emotions of that faraway time, that I was among the last cohort of people who could relate a child's view of those days.

After all, anyone born in or after 1950 had not lived in that special period ranging from the beginnings of World War II to the middle of the twentieth century. In the 1950s, America had begun to dream of a peaceful, prosperous society complete with atomic powered homes. However, the late 1940s had climbed slowly out of the rigors of World War II, while never being able to leave them totally behind.

Of course, as a kid, I never thought in such stark terms. It was only much later that I realized I had lived my childhood in a uniquely challenging era which retained an innocence and simplicity that I would never again experience in my lifetime.

How can I relate accurately things that occurred many decades ago? I can do so with some confidence because of that unique (and mostly mysterious) facility – memory. How is that possible?

Humans have the power to unravel intimate details of the intricate web of life here on Earth, and analyze the composition of distant stars. We are able to discover the secrets of our genes, or take apart the building blocks of atoms.

In doing so, we employ the instrument that makes possible even our thoughts and sensations – that unique, fragile, and stupendously complicated mass of tissue that lies enclosed and protected by the bony cranium – the human brain.

We are only beginning to decipher some of the essential details of this coiled and folded mass of brain cells, revealing at each discovery clues to how the brain manages to accomplish su-ch stunning feats, including the mysterious act of consciousness.

Among the many questions that arise in the study of the brain are those that ask about the precise character of the unique quality we are dealing with here – memory. We all know what the experience of memory is, but beyond this common understanding, from where and by what means do these memories arise? Is every experience "memorized," and only a few recalled?

As I first began to contemplate recording my often intense memories of childhood, the same vivid experiences kept rising up out of my thoughts, like so many buoyant bits floating to the surface of my consciousness.

Where had these been hiding? What allowed them to emerge, sometimes seemingly by themselves, and at other times due to an active effort of my "mind?"

Although I have spent my adult life as a scientist, I shall leave these intriguing questions to other forums. In these pages, I shall simply row out across the lake of my memories, venturing to offer an account of each of the boyhood recollections that have resurfaced again and again over my 82 years on the Earth.

I aim to recount specific memories of my childhood as a young boy, from 1938 to 1950, in Worcester, Massachusetts. I will include only those recollections that are clear and detailed, and I will not invent any embellishments to expand on the incidents.

Our lives recede into the past, even as they advance into the future. The following is an imperfect recording of my early life, written as I prepare for that future's concluding chapter.

MY NEIGHBORHOODS

I have no valid recollection of my first home, an apartment on Tirrell Street, not far from Clark University, where I would study for a Master's degree years later. I say "valid" because I was a mere seven months old when a vicious storm swept in on Worcester, without the early warnings we are now accustomed to receiving.

As an older child, I often heard the story recounted of my playpen that had been picked up in the backyard by the raging storm and lost to the winds. Given my tender age at the time of that incident, it seems impossible that I could have formed a memory of it, but I have a clear image of seeing that playpen through the window, as it was buffeted by The Great New England Hurricane of '38.

Sometime before I was ready for kindergarten, we moved across town to Hadwen Lane. "We" included me, my parents, and my sister Rosemary, two years older than myself. We took up residence in a two-story brown and yellow house. It sat on a rise near the corner facing Pleasant Street, a busy road that stretched from downtown Main Street out westward towards the suburbs of Tatnuck and Paxton.

The area was considered a "Jewish" neighborhood, and featured a synagogue just beyond our house. I suppose there were a number of Jewish families nearby, because I recall looking out the window and watching people walking towards the synagogue. It is sad to admit that my earliest memories were tinged with a message of antisemitism.

I say this because of the clear memory of my mother's voice saying to me, emphatically referring to the Jews, "They like to work for themselves." I hope that my interpretation of her brief remark as being unkind was incorrect After all, she was a gentle and loving woman.

I do not mean to suggest that my mother was seriously prejudiced. She certainly did not avoid Water Street, the locally renowned Jewish district on the other side of town. That street was lined by Jewish-owned businesses. My mother would take me, by bus of course, across town to shop at Widoff's Bakery and Weintraub's Delicatessen.

This early sense of suspicion about "different" people, a reaction that is ingrained in humans by their evolutionary history, was never a dominant theme in my home. This was perhaps because my corner of the world on the western edge of Worcester was a white, predominately Catholic enclave. Life at that time centered around one's neighborhood, and I experienced few "strangers." Most families did not own a car, and the rare travel beyond our immediate confines consisted of a bus ride into the city center.

There were only two notable travel events in our family at that time. My father took a train to Cleveland to apply for a job, and stayed there overnight. That exciting story reverberated for years. An even more adventurous trip was undertaken by my Aunt Anna. I never was told her exact itinerary, but she and a few other female teachers, amazingly, had driven cross country one summer. I would pore over the film reel she brought back, black and white pictures viewed through a magical 3D viewer. She never told us many details about her trip. I blamed her Irish ancestry for her reticence, a characteristic that was shared by her brother Bernard, my father.

* * *

I was just a little kid when we moved to our roomy Hadwen Lane apartment. I had a prized Teddy bear. I gave it the original name "Teddy." It was a small, ginger colored bear with brown glass eyes. I needed that bear in my bed to get to sleep. One evening the bear went missing. I remember a long, widespread search, until he was found in the bushes beside the house.

In our Hadwen Lane driveway, I can see myself and *Billy* jumping off the porch into the drifts after a heavy snowstorm. (The driveway was not used much – we would not have a family car until 1954. I was in high school then, and our first car was a 1938 Buick.) Billy's name is seared into my memory as the kid who my parents held up to me as the example of the perfect boy. He was the son of a dentist, which perhaps gave him a certain panache, and apparently was highly accomplished in some way, even at that young age. I can see clearly to this day what I thought, unfairly, was his smug little face, that of a boy whom I could never hope to match.

I entered kindergarten when I lived on Hadwen Lane. By the time we moved again, first around the corner to Howland Terrace and then several miles to the west to 1351 Main Street, I had completed second grade. I have few memories of those early school days. One is of my very first day of school. I see my mother walking into the schoolroom with me, seating me at a desk on the first row near the wall, and leaving. I put my head down on the desk and cried. Little did I know that, except for a couple of years, I would remain in a school, either studying or teaching, until I was sixty-two.

At the end of that school year, or perhaps it was after completing first or even second grade, I brought home a report card. I can see my mother in the window, as I was standing next to the back porch. She had just returned from the hospital and appeared thin and jaundiced. She seemed to be weeping as she read my report, because it said, "Will not sing alone." Why that should have been devastating news always puzzled me, as I don't think my parents hoped that I would become a vocalist.

And then there was the moment, when walking home from kindergarten with a friend, that I created my first pun. We were in the process of moving from Hadwen Lane around the corner to Howland Terrace. As we were stepping up onto the sidewalk on that corner, we stood on the sewer grate. I said to my friend, "I'm sunk." I added, "I don't know which house to go to." To his eternal credit, he got the joke.

* * *

The kitchen in our Hadwen Lane apartment featured a breakfast nook – a yellow wooden table with benches set into the wall where there was a sunny window. One morning, as we were eating, (I think I was having oatmeal), we heard a repeated clanging. My mother told my father that it was his ride. True enough. It was the trolley, patiently waiting for my father, who apparently had the habit of being a bit late. The trolley man would clang that bell a few times and wait patiently for him to rush out. I recall that my father was wearing a white shirt, one of those that my mother would have starched. I am sure of this because no man who wore a shirt and tie in those days would be wearing anything but a white shirt.

I can picture my father getting onto that trolley. The driver would be sitting at the wheel, in some sort of dark blue uniform, flanked by a set of silver cylinders ready to press out change for the fare. There would be a wire container on the dashboard containing a cake of camphor, about the size of a bar of soap. This was supposed to purify the air, cleansing it of germs. At that time, antibiotics were not readily available. Penicillin, the very first antibiotic was being tested on injured soldiers – with captured Germans acting as the "controls."

The Worcester trolleys disappeared shortly after the scene I am describing, the last one making its final trip in 1945.

Speaking of infectious illness, which was rampant given the lack of available preventives or treatments, I spent a Hadwen Lane Christmas in my bed, recovering from measles. There I was, sitting up in bed listening to the Christmas sounds from the front room. (That term must have come about because those roomy apartments had two rooms beyond the kitchen. The first was often the dining area, and the next was towards the front of the building. Hence, it was the front room.)

Suddenly, my mother came into my room bearing a large box. I tore it open eagerly, and behold, there was

11

a wondrous sight. A fantastic Christmas present – a machine gun, made of some sort of brown cardboard. It could swivel, and had a handle that you could crank and make a loud shooting noise. I sat there, shooting countless Nazis, or maybe Japs, as we all called them – or maybe Nips. What a thrill. Not only that, I also got a small plastic airplane, a P32. There were no moving parts, but my imagination put that plane through many successful dogfights. I kept that plane for many years until it disappeared into that place where still reside the comic books, yo-yos, marbles, baseball cards, and all the other beloved objects that I treasured and remember fondly.

Again, sad to say, in addition to a tinge of antisemitism casting a shadow on my early life, I shared with all my friends an avid interest in the tools of war. The war ended when I was seven years old, and while I didn't spend much time reading newspapers, I could sense all around me the deep hatred of the Germans and the Japanese – the enemy. While we would still occasionally haul out the cowboy and Indian figurines to beat up on the latter, we preferred those games where toy soldiers could aim their rifles and howitzers and other artillery, and kill the hapless foreigners.

* * *

While still at Hadwen Lane, my sister Mary arrived on the scene. By the way, the reader will notice throughout these pages that I seldom mention my sisters. That is simply because my memories of those early years infrequently include them for reasons unknown to me. During these early years, my youngest sister Bernadette was yet to be born. However, Rosemary was two years older than me. Mary entered the family when I was about five.

My mother arrived home from the hospital while I was out in the lot next door, playing with some kids. I ran into the house, and there was my mother, holding a baby wrapped in a blanket. I took one look at the infant and said, "I didn't want a Japanese baby!" and ran outside to continue playing.

My poor parents. Mary had Down syndrome and had arrived home jaundiced. I have no recollection of my mother's reaction to my outburst, but I can imagine it to this day. In the years to follow, I would help with Mary's care, including helping to teach her how to read and tell time. Mary was considered "advanced," in that she could eventually read and write. Her "advancement" never amounted to an ability to live independently. My parents devoted the rest of their lives to supporting and protecting Mary. That continued beyond my parents' lives and ended only with her death in her late sixties. Her last years were spent under the extraordinarily loving, self-sacrificing care of my wife, Eileen.

* * *

The move to Howland Terrace during my kindergarten days was apparently a major transition for my family. We moved into a two-story house. Probably this came about because we needed the room for what had become an extended family. We now numbered my parents, myself, and two sisters, both grandmothers, and Aunt Anna. I would learn years later that Anna, a schoolteacher who never married, helped with the family finances, supplementing my father's humble income as an accountant.

Now there were eight people under my mother's care. It would have been unimaginable for a mother at that time to work outside the home, so this did not conflict with any other job she might have had.

Back then, mothers were uniformly clothed in long, cotton "house dresses." I cannot recall my mother dressed in anything else, along with heavy stockings and "sensible" shoes.

My mother's mother was "Nana." She was a bit on the heavy side, as I have been taught to say. She also wore the house dress uniform. She walked slowly, bent over by osteoporosis. My father's mother was "Gram." In contrast to Nana, Gram was shorter and wiry, and more active. I make no excuses for, nor do I have any explanation of the fact that I have absolutely no recollection of any affection being displayed either by my grandmothers to me, or me to them. They were just there – at least until they both died within two weeks of each other when I was about twelve. After they had passed on, I had my first experience of walking out of the house and leaving it empty.

I cannot recall any instances of sitting on a lap, or hearing a story from them. No dear old Nana or Gram for me. But perhaps they were affectionate in their own way. Who knows? Memories are strangely selective – brief snapshots in our life's album.

There was the time Gram had set up the ironing board. She was busy at work when I walked into the room. I had something to show her. My father had set a mouse trap in the silverware drawer, and I had discovered the dead victim. I thought my grandmother would be happy to see that we had caught the mouse.

Holding it by the tail, I held it out to her.

She took one look, dropped the iron, and ran out of the room, shouting "Mae, Mae!" Apparently, she was calling for my mother, in a panic. I was quite puzzled.

I do not recall any hints of antisemitism in Gram, but she did have a couple of memorable sayings that featured the "N" word. I will not repeat them here.

* * *

We lived on Howland Terrace for only a couple of years, but I did manage to have a few traumatic adventures there. I had acquired a tricycle, and would ride it up and down the large driveway next to our house. Probably the people next door, who were car owners, used the double garage.

One day, I decided to climb up to the garage roof by clambering onto the trash cans hidden behind the cement wall of the garage, and from there, pulling myself onto the roof. After peering around at the new view of the neighborhood, I began to climb down, and promptly fell, bouncing off the trash cans onto the ground. This resulted in a large, bloody gash on my knee (I don't remember which one.) My mother was suitably upset. She dressed the wound with the popular antiseptic of the day, mercurochrome.

That effective bacteria killer was taken off the market in 1998, judged to be "not generally recognized as safe." It probably saved many lives, antibiotics not yet readily available.

My tricycle would prove to be more dangerous than my mounting of the garage. One day, I decided to go for a long ride across the street and down a hill to wherever it might lead. I see myself pedaling to the crest of the hill, and then beginning to pick up speed until I lose control. I hit a raised section of concrete, my tricycle wheel twists, and I fly over the handlebars and land squarely on my face, breaking a front tooth.

I can see the man who had been watering his lawn moving towards me. He washes out my bleeding mouth using the hose, hands me some sort of cloth, and sends me back home. My mother opened the front door and gasped. I suppose I must have seen a dentist after that, but my mind cannot retrieve any more details of that trauma.

* * *

Because the war was still on, there were various precautions taken, which, in retrospect, seem quite pointless. A scene that stays with me took place in our attic. To get into the attic, which was just a large crawl space, one had to climb a ladder, and reaching up, lift a square wooden door, and slide it over onto the attic floor. One could then hoist up onto that floor and crawl around.

In this case, my father and I had gotten up through that opening and crawled over to a small window facing the street. There I saw several men walking slowly along the street. They wore white helmets. My father explained that this was the Civil Defense Patrol, seeing to it that every house had the window shades drawn and all outside lights turned off. This was because we were practicing for an air raid. People in Worcester were convinced that the city was on a short list of sites to be bombed by the Germans.

Why? Well, it was because there were several shoe

16

factories in the city. Since armies needed shod feet, destroying the factories would presumably result in barefooted soldiers trying to march through Europe. I never wondered how those Germans would reach us from far across the ocean.

During that same night, as the Patrol walked the streets, I saw an awesome sight. Rows of large planes flew slowly overhead, lit by powerful searchlights on the ground. They dropped what I was told were sandbags acting as simulated bombs. I often wondered after that if the sandbags had done any damage, and why they would take such a chance of hurting someone.

Those few years on Howland Terrace included several Halloweens. I remember the threat of "tricks" if no "treats" being taken seriously in our neighborhood. One morning, the day after Halloween, our trash cans were perched atop our roof.

That time of year – late October – was marked by the delicious smell of burning leaves. Nothing can ever quite imitate that sweet odor of smoldering leaves, piled in the street. Now, of course, that practice is banned, because of the threat of igniting nearby structures as burning leaves float about, and due to the particles polluting the air.

Those reasons scarcely mattered to the Worcesterites back then. Each yard featured some sort of large can, typically a rusted 55-gallon drum, into which any type of flammable waste was thrown before burning. It made for a neighborhood redolent with the smell of whatever was being burned at that moment. What else to do? There was no recycling, a concept for the distant future. However, papers were somehow used for other purposes

17

as well, because there were periodic "paper drives," usually run by the Boy Scouts as fundraisers. Trash burning certainly afforded a good opportunity for a kid to earn a few cents by numbering that job among the "chores."

A kind woman lived on the far side of the driveway. She invited me onto her back porch one sunny day, and handed me a surprising gift. It was a rubber "Henry," about five inches tall. Henry was a popular comic strip character of the time, and this flexible figure was a perfect, colorful replica of Henry himself. While I remember him as being flexible, it probably was not true rubber, which was in scarce supply during, and for some time, after the war.

I played with this figure constantly, until one day he split in two, and that was that for my most memorable childhood toy.

* * *

Walking home from second grade one day, I was attacked by *Freddy*. Freddy was older, bigger, stronger, and mean. He threw me down on a lawn and proceeded to ensnare me in the dreaded "scissors." He got on top of me, wrapped his legs around my middle, and squeezed so that I could not breathe. I begged him to stop, until I could no longer speak. I felt that I was about to die. Then Freddy released me, stood up, and left. I lay there gasping, glad to be alive.

The next day, I feared that Freddy might assault me again. I hurried towards home, and then spotted Freddy on the opposite side of the street, back about one block. Fortunately, the house I was passing had shrubs along the sidewalk. I quickly ducked behind the scraggly bushes and peered out. Freddy passed by, and never saw me. Maybe that was the end of it. Who knows? I think I would have remembered another attack.

* * *

I am on a long walk with someone, presumably a parent. We make our way past Midland Street School and past a field on our left where a man is flying a kite, or is it some sort of plane? We continue for quite a while, and then come upon a frightening sight. It looks like a castle in miniature, with towers and rough stone walls. That forbidding appearance of what I now know is Bancroft Tower, built in 1900 in memory of George Bancroft, a Worcester born statesman, has never left me.

EARLY CHURCHES

There were two Catholic churches that were significant in my youth. Blessed Sacrament was the first. This church was a walk of just under a mile from our house. We would walk there, of course – we had no car, nor did many others, so the sidewalks were busier than they are in these days of constant auto traffic. I suppose I received First Holy Communion in that large, tan edifice with a tall bell tower, although I do not recollect that event. I do remember the interior ceiling, because I spent many services lying down on the hard, wooden pews, looking upward.

One day, while we were strolling home from Mass – my mother would have been wearing white gloves and some sort of large hat – I came across a treasure on the sidewalk. It was a small tire, a replica of an automobile tire. Perhaps at that same time, or more likely on another Sunday walk, I found a steering wheel. A kid's imagination was all that was needed to enable these to become valuable playthings.

Newton Park lies next to Blessed Sacrament Church. A new store had opened on the corner abutting the park. It boasted a novel approach to buying milk. Instead of waiting for the milkman to deliver bottles to the doorstep, one could stop at this store and buy a gallon of milk, probably in a glass bottle – or perhaps it was still quarts? Anyway, I recall my mother's surprise at this newfangled convenience. Certainly, it was not a Cumberland Farms – they would not open their first store until 1958.

The park was the scene of a most satisfying experience. My parents are standing next to me at the top of a snow-covered hill. I am on my sled, a "Flexible Flyer," telling them that I want to keep sliding, even though I had been there a long time. I could sense that my mother was reluctant. My father said, "Let him get his belly's worth." Down the hill I went, feeling the affection in his decision.

* * *

And then we moved away from Howland Terrace to 1351 Main Street, where I would spend the remainder of my childhood and young adulthood. I would enter the third grade at Gates Lane School, about one-half mile down the hill from my two-story brown, shingled house. I remained at Gates Lane until I had completed the sixth grade. I would then transfer to Woodland Prep, a bus ride away, reserved for "brighter" students. But more on that later.

Our parish would now be Our Lady of the Angels, where I would serve as an altar boy.

1351

We settled into our new home. There was myself, my sisters Rosemary and Mary, Aunt Anna, Nana, Gram, and of course, my parents, Mary (Blanchard) Lee, and Bernard Thomas Lee. While my mother referred to my father as Bernard, I never heard him use her name. He always called her "mother." Nor were there any openly affectionate words exchanged between the two, such as "dear" or "sweetheart." Neither was there ever any affectionate physical contact evident. They were not huggers, that's for sure. I remember my feeling of discomfort years later, when my father met me at the Worcester airport and shook my hand.

However, I always felt that my parents were close, and was never concerned about what seems now, in 2020, to have been an overly formal way of relating. My father's parents were as Irish as Paddy's pig, and my mother's mother was a Celtic Masterson. Perhaps those genes ruled the day, who knows?

When I try to recall where we all slept, the only arrangement I can come up with is a room for my parents, one for my Aunt, another for me, and the fourth for my sisters. All the bedrooms were on the second floor. Where did the grandmothers sleep? I do not know.

Within this string of discrete memories that I am trying to list in a roughly chronological order, I have discovered that at almost no point do they involve my sisters. Certainly, we must have interacted daily, but I find that in most of the scenes that have played and replayed so often in my mind over the decades, my sisters are missing.

* * *

The house needed some repairs when we moved in, but those projects were not critical, and turned out to be work that would be done over a number of years. This would afford my father and I an opportunity to bond, as much as that was possible.

The house stood on a small, grassy lot on the corner of Main Street and Eureka Street. A fence separated us from a large, gray house on the Main Street side, and from another two-story home towards the back of the house. In keeping with the staid personality of the Lees, we never entered either of those houses, nor did we befriend any of the residents, beyond the occasional wave. This may have been compounded by the fact that this was New England, where people tend to keep to themselves to a degree unheard of in other geographical areas.

On the Eureka street side of the property there was a short retaining wall, at the bottom of a slight slope. At the far end of that wall, on the corner away from Main Street, was a large maple tree. Its lowest branch was massive, and curved gently upwards, affording a perfect place for a kid to sit.

A few years after we arrived, my father and I built a wooden latticework fence that formed a patio area, screened off from the eyes of the passing traffic. No carpenter in his right mind would have signed off on that project, but it served its purpose. We poured a cement pad, about ten by ten feet, on the inner side of the new barrier. We now had a private back yard.

The first floor of our home included a living room, a dining room, a kitchen, two pantries, and a small bathroom. A door in the kitchen led to the stairs heading down to the dark cellar. There sat the bulbous body of the furnace, covered with asbestos. Who worried about such things then? Next to the furnace was the coal bin. A small window allowed a bit of light to enter, and was also the entrance through which the "pea" coal was delivered to feed the furnace.

Atop the house was an attic, entered, as in our previous house, through a trap door. It was larger than that other attic, and became the site for storage, including many of my childhood treasures. I still firmly believe that they are there still – the comic books, the baseball cards, the toy soldiers, my Boy Scout stuff. Otherwise, where could they have gone?

The house is still there, but is now a hair salon. The tree was cut down, and the side yard is an asphalt parking lot. Still, maybe they never discovered the attic.

A bit more about the house, which was the major domestic scene of my youth… The large pantry, just off the kitchen, featured several wooden cabinets and a massive, deep soapstone sink where my mother washed the dishes. A window faced the patio area. On the opposite end of the spacious kitchen was a second, smaller pantry that would later become my bedroom when I was a teenager.

On the wall next to that pantry hung a large, framed print of Pope Pius XII. He had his hand raised in blessing, and stared out at us with a serious, almost grim mien. My parents were devoted Catholics. In the early 2000s, when I attended a wake for my cousin Jane, my father's niece, my relatives recounted infrequent visits to our house on Main Street, saying, "When you visited Bernie Lee's house you had better be prepared to get on your knees." They were referring to my parents' habit of getting us all in the kneeling position for the nightly Rosary. Because of that practice, whenever I hear, for example, that something will last one hour, I immediately calculate that to be about four Rosaries.

The kitchen featured a large table with a black and white Formica top, surrounded by wooden chairs. Next to the pantry door stood the white ice box. This was our primitive refrigerator. This contraption was not electrical. It was simply an insulated box. An upper compartment held a large block of ice. As it melted, the water would trickle down the sides of the box and collect in a pan in the lower compartment. This would be emptied into the convenient soapstone sink, just around the corner.

The food sat in the middle section, remaining cool enough to preserve it. And where did that ice come from? More on that later, when I describe the various deliveries we received in those days.

Next to the stove at the back wall was a tall wooden structure that held cabinets at the top. There was a Formica working surface at waist height, and more cabinets below. Among those was a small door that swung outward, revealing a container for flour. My mother was an avid baker, and I was often recruited to help her make the cakes and pies and puddings. Even now, when I am baking, I find myself making those same moves of measuring and mixing that I learned there long ago. I do not think my mother ever allowed either my aunt or grandmothers to cook.

One day, when I arrived home from school, I decided that I needed to retrieve something from the upper cabinets, which were just beyond my reach. I managed to grab onto the door handle and give it a yank. I can still see the entire top section descending on me, as I quickly jumped back amid the tumbling contents.

My mother rushed in, more worried about my safety than the awful mess that I made.

Around the corner from the icebox were the laundry sink and the washing machine. If the dirty items needed additional scrubbing, my mother would get out the washboard – a corrugated glass plate in a sturdy wooden frame – prop it in the porcelain sink, and have at it. Those scrubbed things would go into the machine with the rest of the laundry. After washing, each piece would be squeezed through the mangle.

This was a set of two rollers, closely aligned in a metal frame set above the washer. The wet laundry would be inserted into the separation between the rollers, and the handle would then be cranked to move the item between the rollers, squeezing out the excess water.

My mother would then take the washed laundry out to the back yard and hang it on the clotheslines arrayed around a frame, with four arms holding rows of rope. This could only be done in warm weather. During the winter, she would reach out through the bathroom window and pin the wet items on a long line that stretched between a pulley at the window and another on the fence.

Of course, when the laundry was taken in, it would often be frozen stiff. Some things could be put on wooden racks in the basement. Ohers, such as pants, would stand propped against a wall to thaw. Sweaters could be stretched on a metal frame so they would retain their shape.

In a couple of spots in the kitchen there was a radiator. We used steam heat to warm the house. I can hear the hiss and knocking of those heavy, hollow iron radiators that we learned early on not to touch. In later years, they would be hidden with decorative covers.

Upstairs, there were four bedrooms and a bathroom. The bedrooms occupied the four corners of the house. In the corridor outside the two front bedrooms sat a beautiful mahogany Victrola. It was a record player that one wound up with a crank to spin the record. Then, one would carefully lower the needle. It seems to me that this instrument was seldom used, and I don't know where it ended up. I remember it as a treasured, polished cabinet whose lid hid the workings.

Back downstairs, a rear door led out of the kitchen and into a small storage area from which another door opened out to a couple of steps. Upon exiting the house, to the right was the narrow path leading to the sidewalk along Main Street. To the left, around the corner of the house, was a somewhat wider strip of ground leading to the patio area and the large tree. This area proved to be an ideal spot for playing marbles, and for putting golf balls. For the former, I needed only to scoop out a small indentation for the goal. For the latter, I would dig enough of a hole to insert a soup can, so that the top was flush with the dirt.

I managed to amass a decent collection of marbles by either buying them or trading with my friends. I treasured those marbles, and would admire each one for its luminous colors. I usually played by myself in the backyard, but when I played somewhere else in the neighborhood, I was always sad if I lost some of my valued collection.

The patio was a good spot to stand and throw a ball against the house wall. My mother never complained about what must have been an annoying, thumping racket.

* * *

When we first arrived at 1351, the front door opened onto a small, wooden, roofed porch, fronted by a couple of fieldstone steps held together by cement. My father must have decided that this area needed more protection from the elements. He and I put together six wooden sections, each about 3 feet wide and 8 feet tall. We screwed these onto the frame of the porch, and inserted a door at the top of the steps. Each year, we would laboriously haul the heavy wooden sections out of the cellar, and figure out what the inscriptions meant that were supposed to indicate where each section should be put.

Once, when I was standing on the porch as my father struggled with the heavy wooden sections, my jackknife slipped while I was carving on a stick. I managed to carve out a pretty good slice on my palm. I still have the scar on my right hand. I have another landmark on the same hand that I will describe later when I write about my days at Woodland Prep, where I was sent for the seventh and eighth grades.

While I am on the topic of home repairs, there is one that deserves special mention. When we arrived at 1351, the galvanized water pipes were in bad shape, being quite choked with rust. My father decided, bravely, that we could replace the pipes in the cellar.

Our method was as follows, unencumbered by any professional advice. We would measure several sections of piping, then head down to Webster Square, trailing my red wagon behind. This was about a mile or so away. At Aubuchon hardware we would buy some galvanized pipes, and have them cut and threaded at the ends. We would sometimes need to buy some elbows and connectors as well, along with joint compound. We loaded up the wagon and headed home.

Today, of course, the job would be done with copper pipes, and these would be joined with solder. Back then, it was all galvanized. We would smear some of that joint compound (my father referred to it as "dope") on the threads, and screw one section onto the next. The objective was to end up with a level, straight course of pipes. We ended with a maze of meandering pipes that roughly approximated what we were replacing. We supported this creation with wire hangers attached to the floor beams. We now had a water system that was imperfect, but was at least functional, and afforded us a chance to joke about the sketchy but difficult job we had done. This was a real bonding experience, the likes of which I have repeated many times with my own son – but never again with water pipes. At least we now have the benefit of a Google search to find home maintenance advice.

So far, I have described my home at 1351 Main Street and something of its contents. Now I want to put that house into its context – neighborhood, parish, and city. You might wonder why I would think to include "parish" to portray our locale. Well, at that time, in that most Catholic of cities, if I were to ask another kid where he was from, he might very well say "Saint Peter's" or "Sacred Heart." If someone were to ask me, I would reply "Our Lady of the Angels."

So here I am, walking out of the front door, down the steps, between a short row of yew bushes, and onto the sidewalk. Let's make this a summertime stroll. I'm wearing cotton pants with a belt (never shorts – we never saw any of those), a t-shirt (white, of course, no lettering or pictures), and high top sneakers. Being hot weather, my hair is cut in the form of a "butch." This involves a thorough clipper cut, so that the hair is very short and stands up straight on the top of the head, assisted by a liberal application of "butch wax."

In front of me is Main Street, a busy thoroughfare that runs all the way from the far end of the city's downtown to the westward, out towards the border with the town of Leicester. About three miles from downtown, Main Street passes our brown house on the corner of Eureka Street. There would usually be only a handful of cars traveling by. Occasionally, we would see a streamlined orange and black express bus, the Shortline, streaking by. That sight always scared me.

Turning right, I head down the street towards Webster Square. I look ahead, and can see all the way down a gentle hill to my school, Gates Lane, situated on the opposite side of the street. I cross Eureka Street. On the corner opposite my house is Kaplan's grocery store, owned and operated by my friend Arthur Kaplan's father. The family lived over the store.

Beyond Kaplan's there are three or four three-deckers. These structures were a very common means of efficiently housing three families. The owner often occupied the first floor. Each level held a roomy apartment. The back door of each level was located on a porch that looked out over the back yard. From there one entered a kitchen. A bedroom extended from the kitchen. Moving ahead, one came to a dining room, with an entry to a second bedroom, and beyond that was the "front room," "sitting room," or "parlor." There was a door leading from there out to stairs heading down to the front door.

Being afraid of heights, I was always grateful when a friend lived no higher than the second floor. However, I was hanging around one day with a kid on Henshaw Street – the next one down from Eureka – and we decided to test the urban legend that cats always land on their feet when they jump or fall from a high point.

We grabbed a local cat, and brought it to the third floor. We unceremoniously dropped it over the porch railing. We watched as it plummeted downward. The cat landed squarely on its paws and scampered off. We felt satisfied that we had performed a successful experiment.

Moving on down the street, I cross Henshaw. On my right, as I begin to cross, is the barber shop, with plants in the window. On the opposite corner of Henshaw Street is Sal's drug store, where they have a soda fountain. When I describe my paper route adventures, Sal's is where I will spend some of my earnings on delicious ice cream cones.

Next to Sal's is Morris' Market, while across Main Street sits the E.T. Smith Company, a small food store. My father worked for this company before he became a Worcester City employee. So, within one block, there were three food stores. There were no supermarkets then, allowing each of these to do a brisk business.

E.T. Smith's sat on the corner of Sylvan Street. If one were to walk up that street a short way and turn left, one would see the home of Robert Goddard, the famous inventor of the rocket, literally the father of the era of space exploration. The closest I ever got to him was seeing his wife sweeping their front porch.

Moving down past Morris' Market, I come to a display of gravestones in front of a dealership. Beyond that are a few houses, then Cleveland Ave, a few more homes, and we have reached the bottom of the hill. In keeping with my practice, I am naming only the streets that I can remember, and not relying on the internet to refresh my recollections.

There is a brown and yellow house at the bottom of the hill, where a friend lives. Looking back, I assume he must have had a Canadian-American name, so we naturally called him "Frenchy." I don't remember him minding that. Perhaps he enjoyed it, because kids, at least then, appreciated being given a nickname. When I joined the Boy Scouts, I became "Tilly," and later was called "Skids." At least it means someone is paying attention to you.

I then arrive at a large, scrubby, wooded area, perhaps five or six acres in size. This was a great place for adventures.

It was crisscrossed with paths, and included enough vegetation to afford hiding places for licit and forbidden activity. (It is now a large shopping mall, and the traces of those adventures lie under a broad sheet of asphalt.)

Fronting the woods on the Main Street side is the wildly popular "Fish and Chip," which also serves as a well-stocked penny candy store. The store specializes in delicious fish and chips, doled out to long lines of customers on Fridays, particularly in Lent. Most people in the area being Catholic, and seeing as how one could not eat meat on any Friday of the year, one would make the sacrifice of forgoing the pleasure of a piece of roast beef or steak for the crispy deliciousness of deep fried fish, served with crunchy French fries.

On the side of Main Street directly opposite the Fish and Chip stands Gates Lane School, a large, two-storied brick edifice where I attended grades three to six. On either side of the school are the dirt and gravel school-yards – allowing boys on one side, girls on the other.

Directly behind Gates Lane is a patchy, wooded hill, leading up to a large horse barn and farm. To the left, as one faces the school, is Bennett Field, the scene of our baseball games. There were the official interschool games in the Spring, and many more pickup games throughout the Summer and Fall.

I continue my stroll past the school. A few houses and three-deckers later I have arrived at Our Lady of the Angels Church. This is an imposing, sand colored stone Catholic church, fronted by a broad set of stairs leading up from the sidewalk. In the rear is an imposing bell tower, and off to the side is the rectory and parish school building.

In that era, many Catholic parishes had their own grade schools, complete with nuns, and supported (paid for) by the parishioners.

Let's stop here, because to go further takes us into Webster Square. I will come back to a description of that area when I recount adventures located there.

Returning to 1351, imagine that I take a left turn when exiting the house and head towards Leicester, the small town just west of Worcester. This direction was seldom explored by myself and my friends. Two blocks away was Grandview Ave, scene of many a basketball game played in the street. However, we seldom strayed further down Grandview, which ended on Stafford Street, a thoroughfare I always regarded as a forbidding vicinity. Stafford headed east to Webster Square, and to the west it began to climb sharply to become "Dead Horse Hill."

However, we did occasionally go beyond Grandview, along Main Street, up to the paper mill. Behind the mill was a swift stream, coursing angrily through dense, sinister woods. Depending on the specific product the mill was making on that day, the stream would be variously colored – green, or red, or blue, etc. – and smelling like bleach. So much for hazardous waste disposal back in the forties. I can remember a sense of danger and toxins in those woods, and didn't venture there often.

My house stood on the corner of Main and Eureka Streets. I didn't have much to do with Eureka Street at that time. There were only a couple of kids I knew down along there. A few doors down, there was *Jimmy*, and further on, *P*, who was in Scouts with me, and would meet with a tragic early death. The phrase "I knew" indicates an important distinction to a kid. There were your "friends" as well as other kids who were only acquaintances. Friends did stuff with each other, and acquaintances might interact familiarly with you, but that was it. The difference might be based simply on a disparity in age, or something more complicated, like the fact that you didn't share mutual friends.

There was one other person, only a few houses down on Eureka Street, with whom several of us had a memorable interaction. *Glen* was a man of indeterminate age, who appeared to have some physical disability like asthma, or possibly something worse. He was small, wizened, and had a squeaky voice. His large house featured a grassy side yard. This served as a good spot for pickup games of various sorts – touch football, kickball, stickball – so that is probably how we got to meet him.

Somehow, for reasons that have faded from my memory, Glen convinced us to build a pen in the woods up behind Hendy's field. This was to house geese, which he said we would raise. He must have given us supplies, as well as the geese. We built the darn thing, and took turns caring for the birds. What was their fate? My memory bank does not contain the answer. Our parents knew nothing about this adventure, any more than they knew of almost anything we did. Once you were out of the house, and into the neighborhood with its shifting mix of kids out there playing, you were in your private world.

One block down from Eureka was Henshaw Street. The barbershop and the drug store sat on the corners of Henshaw and Main, and the street was full of possibilities. There was stickball in the empty lot, curb ball in front of Davy's three-decker, or touch football down near the Fleming's house. Behind Davy's three-decker there was a dusty, empty lot, featuring a few 55-gallon barrels for burning trash. It was a good spot for shooting cans and bottles with BB guns. I was never allowed to have a gun, but some of my friends (and foes) did, so that didn't matter.

My world at that time was basically the space within which I could walk. There were no "soccer moms" or drop offs and pickups, for the simple reason that most people did not yet own a car. However, because walking was such a given, my activities encompassed a radius of about two miles. All I wanted or needed was within those miles – school, church, grocery stores, drug stores, barber shops, movies, the doctor – and most importantly, my friends.

BOY SCOUTS

I don't recall any Cub Scout organizations at that time, but certainly I became an interested and active Boy Scout at an early age. Now, in the 21st century, I tend to regard the Scouts as a kind of paramilitary organization, not to mention a possible haven for adults who might be inclined to take advantage of young boys.

However, as a kid, I loved the Scouts, and was not aware of the latter problem. I took Scouting very seriously, as I did everything else at that age. I followed the rules, and assumed that everyone else would be inclined to do the same. I wore the uniform per the requirements, worked carefully on merit badges, showed up at meetings, and figured that the other kids would do the same.

That would not be the case. Scouting was my first memorable example of the fact that rules, norms, and the conviction that one should always be "good," was not equally shared. My mother saw to it that I had the correct uniform, clean and pressed. I was punctual, completed the assignments, and lined up at the command of the Scoutmaster. So why didn't some of the other guys do the same? Why would they show with a wrinkled shirt, half untucked? Why did they fool around, laughing and joking when it was obvious that they were supposed to be at attention? What was wrong with them?

We were Troop 99, from Our Lady of the Angels Parish. To get to the meetings, I would walk down along Main Street all the way to Webster Square. We met in the local American Legion Hall, in front of which stood a large magnolia tree that was covered with magnificent pink blossoms each Spring. That Legion Hall is long gone, replaced by a Burger King. Construction of that franchise required cutting down the magnolia.

I have clear memories of our leader, Scoutmaster *Henry*. He was probably about 50, of medium height, with an expanding waist, thinning black hair and a sinister, pencil-thin mustache. I was fascinated by the knife that he carried on his belt. It was long-bladed, with a yellow handle, and it was in a brown leather sheath that hung low at his right hip. It was so cool, and commended my respect.

In the end, *Mr.* proved to be a rather ineffective leader, despite the impressive knife. As an example, I can point to the matter of merit badges. One advanced through the ranks of Scouting from the lowly Tenderfoot to the ultimate rank, Eagle Scout, by accomplishing specific tasks that would earn small cloth patches – merit badges – that could be displayed on a sash draped across the uniform. A quick glance at any uniformed Scout would immediately tell one the level of his achievement.

Mr. was adept at promising to work with us on various merit badges, but those promises were not always kept. My enthusiasm peaked when he announced, "Boys, we are going to work on the nature badge, and for that we are going to turn around (he often used that phrase), and we are going to get a big barrel. Then we get a long plank, and set that barrel up at the edge of a pond, and balance the plank up against the barrel. Then we will put some bait in the barrel. Turtles will smell the bait and they will crawl up the plank. It will tip and spill those turtles into the barrel."

It was never clear to me exactly how that plank system would work, or how all this might lead to a nature merit badge, but the promised project had me excited. *Mr.* periodically repeated his promise of that awesome turtle barrel technique, but it went no further. Somehow, he turned our attention to other things.

As for those badges, I did manage to advance to the rank of First Class, three ranks below Eagle. The Scout troop broke up as we got older, but I never had any regrets about not having had the chance to try for that exalted rank. I always knew that such a feat would never be possible, because an Eagle Scout was required to swim one mile. I never learned to swim well, but I did try.

I do want to record that I had plenty of fun in Scouts, especially when we went camping, despite the stresses of those adventures. I suppose one objective of getting us out into nature was to toughen us up, as well as to teach us some practical skills. However, this aim seems to have required us to head out into the woods regardless of weather conditions. We would camp in rain, snow, and below freezing temperatures.

Given the superb camping equipment of today, that might seem the ideal time to break out the waterproof tents, the Gore-Tex rain gear, or the down parkas. No such luck in the 1940s. A pair of us would be given two Army surplus canvas pup tent halves that we had to button together. At the campsite, after clearing the ground of debris (usually leaving a few rocks that we would discover in the middle of the night immediately under our backs), we would put up the tent. Then, using our foldable foxhole shovels – also Army surplus – we would dig a channel around the base of the tent in the vain hope that, if the rains came, the water would glide off the tent and be carried away. In reality, if it did rain, the tents would become saturated, and would begin to drip into the interior.

We would lie on a "ground sheet," a thin piece of material on which to place our sleeping bags. If we happened to be camping in the winter – a favorite practice to test our endurance – we would add a blanket inside our wool "mummy cases." These were zippered, narrow, wool sacs shaped like an Egyptian sarcophagus. No goose down insulated comfy bags for us. However, we could make it to sunrise if we were careful to wear a hat (Navy surplus), gloves, and wool socks, along with our clothes and winter coats.

Despite all that, I remember only the sense that I was having fun, sharing these hardships with my friends. We could not have felt deprived of better equipment because it did not yet exist. I still have two souvenirs from those far-off adventures – an aluminum mirror and a waterproof match holder. The latter had a rough exterior so that one could strike and ignite the perpetually dry wooden matches. Carrying matches was considered a necessity, along with a dime in case we had to make an emergency call – provided we could find a phone booth.

Once a year, we would have an extended camping experience, this time in the relative comfort of Treasure Valley. This was the local Boy Scout summer camp where we spent two weeks, mercifully not in small tents. Instead, there were large tents complete with wooden platforms, each with four cots. As soon as we arrived for our stay, we would be told to break out those surplus shovels and dig a latrine just outside the back of the tent. This trench, called a "tilly," was about six feet long and about two feet deep. At the bottom of the trench we placed a layer of stones and gravel. We hung several large cans full of water on a line stretching the length of the tilly. We punched a small hole in the bottom of each can and inserted a small stick, so that the water slowly dripped out onto the rocks.

Having labored to produce this masterpiece, we then had the privilege of using the tilly as a place to pee, thus creating a faint odor of urine, particularly evident at night. There was a standard outhouse nearby for other wastes.

Because my name is Tom Lee, which can be easily shortened to TLee, I soon became known as Tilly. You might think that I would be upset by such mockery, but giving a kid a nickname means he gets attention, and that usually is preferable to not being noticed at all.

At summer camp, we were expected to become proficient at such skills as learning how to tie various knots, shoot with a bow and arrow, and use a knife with care. Having a knife at that time was a necessity, not because we really needed to walk around with a four or five-inch sharp knife in a sheath attached to our belts. It was considered the cool thing to do, so we all dutifully took safety lessons to earn our "totin' chip." With that document, we could tote those knives with permission at camp. When camp was over, we tended to carry jack-knives, or even switchblades. Why? Well, a kid might need a knife – you just never knew.

Jackie, a fellow Scout, apparently had forgotten his totin' chip lessons when he ran off after a buddy through the woods, waving his hunting knife as though he was going to attack him – all in fun, of course. The fun ended when Jackie tripped over a fallen log, fell, and the knife entered his cheek and continued upwards behind his eye.

Luckily, he escaped serious injury, and was a temporary hero because he bore an admirable facial scar, too faint to be disfiguring, but noticeable enough to allow a bit of bragging.

Another serious accident befell one of our Scouts during a paper drive. Each year, the Boy Scouts in various troops would be driven around their sections of the city to collect newspapers. This was advertised widely, and people would save their newspapers and leave them on the sidewalk. On this occasion, *Tommy* was sitting, dangling his legs off the back of a pickup truck during the paper drive. As the truck accelerated, he fell off. He was rewarded with a concussion.

That might have taught us a lesson, but we rarely encountered pickup trucks. I certainly never rode in one as a kid. I did, however, get a chance to ride in the rumble seat of someone's car. This was a two-person seat that folded out from the car trunk, and allowed passengers to ride almost as though they were in a convertible. They were last made in 1939.

* * *

The camp was divided into sites for various troops from Worcester. Our counselors got the bright idea that we should challenge the adjoining troop to a contest. They made this a wrestling match, but with our side gaining a competitive advantage. This was to be attained by having us strip to our waists, greasing our upper bodies with butter, charging into the next campsite, and attacking the campers.

The advantage would be that because we were greased, and therefore slick, our opponents would be unable to hold onto us, and their unbuttered bodies would be fair game. As it turned out, as soon as we grappled with an opponent we all ended up on the ground. This meant that any buttered surface immediately became covered with dirt, and the winner was determined only by the abilities of whatever kid we had picked as an opponent.

The fight was soon called off. I was disappointed only in the sense that I had managed to almost subdue my opponent, which would have marked the only time I ever managed to engage in a struggle without being on the losing end.

I was unable to stand out in any specific physical endeavor, but, being an avid reader, I did manage to wield a pretty good vocabulary. This backfired once. A kid announced that we all had to go to a meeting later that day. I reassured everyone within earshot that the meeting was not "mandatory." I was immediately mocked with shouts of "Did you hear what Tilly just said?" and "Say it again." I realized at that moment that there was indeed a class system in America, and I belonged to the upper class.

At Treasure Valley, besides the emphasis on knife safety and the ability to tie a proper sheepshank, half hitch, or square knot, great care was taken to keep us safe in the water. The prized privilege of using a canoe was allotted only to boys who had demonstrated adequate swimming skills. I certainly was not among that number. The daily swims in the shallow and supervised area, always with a buddy, were all I could handle.

The buddy system never made much sense to me because it was obvious that, if my buddy got in trouble in the water, I would be of little use in helping him out of his predicament. My aquatic skills extended to a brief spasm of dog paddling to the nearest stable object.

That makes this next incident even more problematic. One day, as a couple of my friends and I were walking near the pond, one of them, I think it was *Franny*, told us that his family had a camp down at the far end. He suggested that we sneak down there and use the family canoes. Sneaking and canoeing were not part of my repertoire, but I agreed in order to be accepted into this adventurous gang. Off we went out of the camp property and down to the cabin. I began to question my decision as the other guys began to light up firecrackers along the way.

We got to the cabin and jumped into the canoes. No sooner had we gotten underway, when we spotted a couple of canoes headed towards us from the waterfront, paddled by what looked like counselors. We jumped out of the water, and after a quick consultation, decided to split up and head back through the woods. I thought of a better idea, and strolled up to the road leading back to the camp entrance. As I walked nonchalantly through the gateway, I was immediately apprehended by a waiting official, who marched me down to the camp leader's office.

I was relieved when, after a few chiding remarks, he told me to report back to him the next morning. I showed up as directed, expecting only a tongue lashing. Instead, he informed me that I was to be sent home. I had to go back to the tent site, pack my Army surplus duffle bag, and head home, driven by a counselor.

I had to give him directions to my house. When we got near the Church I told him that I lived in that location. He dropped me off, and after he drove away, I hastened into the Church to implore God to spare me from my parents' wrath. By the way, this visit would not be possible today, as churches are typically locked tight except when services are held. In those days, however, the doors were kept open, and there would be a steady trickle of people making a "visit."

After my supplications, I wended my way homeward, dragging my big khaki bag. When I came in the door, my mother was shocked, worrying that I was ill. She was easy enough to placate because she was relieved that I was in one piece. My father, however, happened to be home as well, and he was furious. His anger was fueled by his concerns about me going out in a canoe, because he knew that I was a prime drowning candidate. I was banished to my room without supper. That was never much of a punishment because I could count on my mother to carry a tray of food up the stairs to my bedroom later in the evening. I was on my best behavior for quite a long while after that episode. I was never to return to Treasure Valley.

RELIGION

The holy, Roman, Catholic, and apostolic Church was at the center of our lives. The city of Worcester was a city filled with churches – mostly Catholic. A view of the city skyline is still dotted with church steeples. Our parish, Our Lady of the Angels, was one of the largest and most imposing churches of which I was aware, except for the Cathedral in downtown Worcester.

Pretty much everyone I knew wore at least one religious symbol, as though these were Catholic dog tags. These typically took the form of a "miraculous medal," a small silver, oval medal bearing a figure of Mary, mother of God, and/or a scapula or two. There were the green or the brown scapulas, cloth squares suspended on a strand of that same material. On each square was a religious picture. It could get to be quite a tangled knot around one's neck when two or three strands of this religious bling collided.

One other religious symbol, very much part of our lives then, was the Rosary. "Saying" the Rosary was a nightly devotion in our house for years. There was a period when we would all kneel in the living room and listen to those prayers being recited on the radio.

My parents saw to it that we were well supplied with rosaries, which come in a variety of materials – glass, stone, wooden, etc. They made ideal birthday or

Christmas gifts. My mother and father were good, God-fearing people. (Strange that we were taught to fear God, who, we are told, loves us so much.)

The only Protestant church I knew was near Our Lady of the Angels. I regarded it as a somewhat mysterious and slightly dangerous place. We would be warned from the pulpit that if we needed to attend a funeral or wedding there, we must not participate in the liturgy by, for example, standing or kneeling at the appropriate times. To do so would have been to indicate that we considered their ceremonies as valid. This came under the category of "giving scandal."

During those years in the 1940s, as well as for the rest of their lives, my parents were regular and devoted churchgoers. I am not sure why that did not include attending daily Mass, a common practice in those days. I would be more apt to be in Church in the early mornings because I was an altar boy.

That privilege came with some rather rigorous preparation. We recruits would report to the rectory after school. That imposing white building standing next to Our Lady of the Angels Church was staffed by the pastor, Monsignor Lynch, and the two young curates, red-haired Father Harty, and neatly combed and polished Father LeBeau, along with a housekeeper.

The latter priest would lead us through drills on the Latin responses that we would have to memorize. All Masses were said in Latin, and altar boys, two per Mass, had to assist the celebrant, not only by responding to his prayers. The duties also included carrying the heavy book from one side of the altar to the other at the appropriate time, and ringing the bells at the consecration.

At a more elaborate "High" Mass, held at funerals or weddings, we would also be in charge of the thurible, a golden container suspended by chains, in which we would ignite a small disc of charcoal. The thurible, also called a censer, would hang next to the altar. At specific intervals, we would hand the thurible to the priest, and offer him a container of incense – the incense boat. He would carefully take a scoop of incense and place it on the glowing charcoal. It would ignite quickly, and the priest would wave it about as the sweet smoke wafted to the rafters as a symbol of prayers rising to the heavens.

There would be Hell to pay for the altar boy who had not lit the charcoal carefully, thus not allowing the incense to burn, or one who forgot to grab that thurible at the right time. Our challenges were amplified by having to carry the heavy book at specific times to the priest, and hold it up at the proper angle so that he could read it.

These High Masses were occasions for us to wear special red cassocks instead of the usual black, as well as lacy surplices. The whole business required the services of intelligent, responsible boys. I was considered to be one of those. My status was evident when I was released from Gates Lane, my public school near the church, whenever there was a funeral that required my assistance.

My mother could be counted on to faithfully wash and starch my white surplice. I never gave a thought to the work that chore entailed, let alone all the other laundry, cleaning, and cooking that went on every day in the life of the faithful "housewife" in her house dress and sensible shoes. Of course, the idea of my mother, or any other mother I knew in those days working at a job outside the house, the way men did, or driving a car to pick us up or drop us off anywhere, would have been a mad fantasy.

One early morning, after I took my clean surplice from the closet, I headed off down the street towards church and the seven o'clock daily morning Mass. I was walking along the sidewalk a couple of blocks from my house. I was approached by a spotted Dachshund, one of those animals we called "firehouse dogs."

I bent over to pet him. He leapt up and took a healthy bite out of my right shoulder. Back to the house I scrambled to my mother. It was easy to get some medical attention for me – our family doctor lived very close to where the traumatic incident had taken place. He cleansed the wound, put in a couple of stitches, my mother paid him in cash, and I was declared fixed. Years later, it occurred to me that it might have been the doctor's dog.

My other surplice-associated memory involves a fellow altar boy, *Tommy*. One day, he and I were in our liturgical outfits, busily cleaning and refilling the racks of devotional candles in front of the Blessed Mother's altar. In addition to the large, ornate main altar, churches then had two "side altars" flanking the central altar. On one side, the small altar was typically dedicated to Mary, while the other honored Saint Joseph.

Each altar featured a metal stand full of small beeswax candles housed in red glass containers. Parishioners would frequently "make a visit" to the church during the day, and often light one of these candles. There would be a box on this stand where the faithful would put coins to pay for the candles. I think it was probably ten cents or so. Off to the side of this array of fifty or sixty small "vigil lights" was a small collection of much larger candles.

These were more expensive, but they would burn much longer than their smaller counterparts, and presumably carry a lot more clout. Anyway, Tommy and I were busily scraping out the remains of the old candles, and replacing them with new ones, when Tommy's surplice sleeve got too close to a burning candle, and the starched material ignited. He stood there for a moment as the flames began to billow. I quickly began to beat at his surplice with my bare hands, and was able to quench the flames. We walked back to the sacristy and reported the incident.

Now here is probably the reason that this incident has stayed with me over the years. The fire was not the most memorable part of the drama. It is the fact that, as I stood there with scorched hands, no one, including Tommy, uttered a word of thanks for my heroics. It was as though nothing had ever happened.

Am I making too much of this incident? Perhaps, but I can relate that, one day, *Tommy* would pursue me with a BB gun and shoot me between the eyes. I will include that incident when I elaborate on my fishing adventures.

There were several other stressful obligations for us altar boys. Before each Mass, one of us would have to walk out to the altar and light the candles. This was accomplished using a long metal rod with a wooden handle. Mounted on the rod was a narrow tube in which there was a wick. One would push the wick out of the aperture at the top of the tube by pushing on a tab at the base. That wick could then be lit before entering the sanctuary. We would carry that rod in one hand, while shielding the flame with the other, to keep it lit. Once in a while, to our chagrin, the flame would go out, and we would have to march back to the sacristy to light it again. That seems unimportant, but if this were a Sunday Mass, we were very aware of several hundred worshipers watching our bungling.

Then, when lighting the candles, there was the problem of getting the flame on the lighter to contact the wick on the candle. Those wicks were hidden by a gold band at the candle apex. Sometimes we just could not make that happen. The priest, or even another altar boy who imagined himself to be more skillful, would come out and get the job done. This was always quite an embarrassment.

Even trickier was assisting with communion. The faithful would approach the altar rail and kneel in a long row. The priest and an altar boy would start at the end of the rail in front of the Saint Joseph side altar. The altar boy would station himself at the priest's right elbow, and as each host was given to the recipient, the altar boy would step backwards towards the next communicant. This required a certain level of dexterity, because each host distribution required the priest to remove a host from the chalice and dexterously drop it onto the person's tongue. Meanwhile, the altar boy would hold a golden plate, the paten, held by means of a slender handle, under that person's chin, lest the host accidentally not make it to its intended destination.

Given all the moving parts involved, it is no wonder that during the distribution of dozens of hosts, which by the way also involved the incantation of the words, "Corpus Christi" by the priest, and the recipient's response, "Amen," something might go awry. For example, if the host were to fall, and the altar boy did not catch it on the paten, it might make its way to the floor.

This engendered a great fuss. After all, this was decades before the faithful were allowed to accept the host in the hand before consuming it. In the 1940s, the mere idea of doing that would be shocking. After this accident, the priest would place a linen cloth at the site so that after Mass there would be a proper cleanup. The altar boy, if he were deemed to have been careless, would be given the appropriate lecture, the intensity of which would vary among the parish clergy.

The priests in our parish were aided by a group of nuns. I never had much to do with them or the parish grammar school because I went to public school. However, I was required to attend religious education classes each Saturday morning, certainly not a favorable time to be sitting in church. This was referred to as "catechism." All the grades would assemble at their assigned spots in the large church, the result being that we could hear the scattered lessons being given all about us.

The nuns would go through the various sections of the Baltimore catechism, which by the time we were eleven years old we could recite from memory. One specific scene has stayed with me all these years. I was sitting in a pew, near a confessional, as the sister warned us about sin, explaining that it offended and literally hurt God. I accepted that as fact, the way I accepted everything we were told. Suddenly, I was overwhelmed with astonishment that anyone, knowing this, could possibly ever sin. I was deeply puzzled by the notion that, given the stakes, people would do such a terrible thing. Of course, at that age in my life, I had very little experience of the variety of temptations one might meet with later in life.

Each Sunday, there would be a Mass which the children were obliged to attend. We sat in assigned sections according to our grade. A nun would station herself near the central aisle, and at the points in the ceremony when we were expected to kneel or stand, she would stand and operate a wooden device that would create a loud click. At that signal we would perform the required movement. She would also usher us up to the communion rail. Back then, there was always an ornate railing between the body of the church and the altar area. Only priests and altar boys were allowed beyond that barrier.

Certainly, no women were permitted to enter that sacred space. Speaking of women, as altar boys we would occasionally be asked to assist the priest in a "churching." This was a ceremony, performed at the Blessed Mother side altar during the day, without witnesses, in which a woman who had recently given birth was asked to kneel at the altar rail, with her head covered, and receive a blessing that was intended to cleanse her from any taint of the sexual connotations of having conceived and given birth. The young altar boy stood by, holding a candle, illuminating the darkness suggested by this absolution.

I have already mentioned the names of the three priests at Our Lady of the Angels. One afternoon, as I was making a visit, I came across Monsignor Lynch, a large, balding Irish-American, chatting with a man in the church vestibule. To my amazement, Monsignor Lynch was speaking French. It seemed quite exotic and somehow slightly suspicious to me.

The two curates, Fathers Harty and LeBeau, were a study in contrasts. The former was a somewhat irascible Irish-American, whose fingers were yellowed by his smoking habit. Father LeBeau, on the other hand, was as neat and "as clean as a whistle" as Gram would say. His name suggests to me now that he was of French ancestry, but that never occurred to me at the time. He was very kind to us altar boys, and we looked forward to chatting with him after Mass.

Father Harty was not chatty. In fact, he was often steamed after the ceremony was over. Often, a parishioner or two, positioned towards the rear of the church, would decide to take an early exit before Father would give the final blessing, descend the altar steps, and proceed into the sacristy.

Woe to the errant parishioners he spied sneaking out a bit prematurely. Father Harty would turn, stop, stare in the direction of the offenders, and give them a substantial piece of his mind. That happened often. It turned out that my parents did not care for this irascible cleric. This was not because of his temper, but because he had developed a friendship with several men in the parish, and it was said that he and these friends would get together each week to play cards, smoke, and possibly drink.

This was not acceptable behavior for a Catholic priest, at least according to my parents. This incident serves as an example of the difficult lives these men endured. There was an abundance of priests then. A priest, once he had settled into a parish and gotten to know many of the parishioners, and, heaven forbid, developed some human friendships, periodically would be abruptly told to uproot himself from those comfortable surroundings, and move to another parish to begin again.

THE THINGS WE WORE

The only time I can recall ever being preoccupied with my clothes was during the fifth grade. *Donald* sat in the front row of Miss Goodspeed's class in Gates Lane School. Donald and I had somehow developed a kind of competition regarding our hair, and this challenge came to extend to our clothes.

He often would arrive in class before me, so that when I entered the classroom through the front door I would immediately check on his hair and outfit. I favored a well brushed head of hair topped off with a modified pompadour, effected by combing the front section up and towards the back. He had blond hair, and had enough curl in it to create an attractive tangle. I do not know how we were able to compare one style with the other, but I was conscious of at least "defeating" him more than once.

I dressed in the style of the day – pants and some sort of shirt, flannel in cool weather, or short-sleeved in warmer periods, the latter being called a sport shirt. The pants were either corduroy or plain cotton, if they were what we now call "jeans," we would refer to them as "dungarees."

During my Donald competition, I was careful to sport my "cowboy" belt, a narrow leather belt in which there were embedded, about two inches apart, colored glass rhinestone-like pieces. Take that, Donald.

My clothes, like those of my peers, would sometimes wear or even rip. There was no immediate replacement as might be the case today. Instead, my mother would either stitch the injured area by hand, or sew on a patch using her Singer sewing machine. It was a common sight to see a kid with pants that had suffered a serious tear show up with that tear neatly, and obviously, repaired. It did help that my mother could skillfully put a patch on the inside of a pants leg, so that only the small stitches showed.

The same principle applied to footwear. Brown leather shoes were meant for school or church, while play required sneakers. Both types, unless we outgrew them, at which time they were handed down if there was a sibling, were repaired if needed. Shoes were made with what seems to have been poor quality bottoms, because we often would wear a hole through the sole. This could be treated, at least temporarily, by cutting out a piece of cardboard which was inserted into the shoe to cover the hole.

This worked fairly well, but often the cardboard would shift, and we would begin to feel bits of dirt and gravel working their way inside. That could lead to a trip downtown to the shoe repair shop, by bus of course. That site featured a series of open wooden sections about waist high, each containing a chair. One would enter and take a seat. A worker would come over, take the wounded shoe, and walk over to a machine where he would put on a new sole. The heel might be worn down along the edges, so he might hammer on a replacement. The repaired shoe would be returned, and you would be good to go. Often, the new soles would be slick and slippery, so we would scrape them along the sidewalk to scuff up them up and make it safer to walk.

This scenario reminds me of another one of those kids whom I remember with disdain, through no fault of his own. My father had a friend, *George*. He had a son whose name I cannot recall, but who has remained painfully real to me all these years. This kid apparently had learned something about the art of shoe repair, and his father, on more than one occasion, impressed my father when describing those skills. This message was passed on to me, and I have never been able to shake the sense of inadequacy caused by this kid's cleverness. I never met him, but I pictured him sitting at that last, with a few nails hanging from his mouth, as he carefully replaced a shoe sole.

As far as the sneakers were concerned, they were black high top types. They were even more apt to wear out than the shoes, especially because they were used for playing outside. For a time, I had a pair of Joe Lapchick sneakers, named after one of the original Boston Celtics players. Sneaker damage was rare on the rubbery bottoms, but was common along the edge, where the tops connected to the bottoms. You would be running around, let's say, on a dirt basketball court, or maybe across a field, when small stones would work their way through the gaps. You would be forced to stop, take off the sneaker, and shake out the gravel.

One night, as we were coming back from fishing, we were walking down a hilly path through a cow pasture. We disturbed a cow, which reared up and scared us enough to make us start running. I happened to be wearing sneakers, one of whose bottom was ready to separate from the top. It did so as we were galloping down the hill, and as my foot became exposed, I stepped into a pile of manure, known to us as a "cow flap." Being kids, we just thought it was hilarious.

During the warmer months, we would wear white t-shirts. These never displayed any symbols or messages. They were simply blank slates that would have to wait many years before someone had the bright idea to decorate them.

The t-shirt would mark a significant stage in my days as a kid. One summer day, I was running up the sidewalk from Henshaw Street towards home. When I arrived at my front yard and jumped over a small bush near the front of the house (I used to think that passing drivers would see me and remark at my athleticism), I was suddenly struck with a stunning revelation. I was skinny! I don't mean slim, or slender, or rangy. I mean the kind of bony, weak skinniness that my t-shirt could not hide.

I never fully recovered from that momentary insight. It would lay dormant somewhere in the back of my mind for years until someone might say something like, "Yeah, my friend is really tall like you, but he's big," with heavy emphasis on the "big." And there I would be again, a skinny kid in a t-shirt.

To add insult to injury, when I was a fifth-grader, I was selected to model the new basketball uniform at a parents' night. There I was, skinny me, draped in a baggy basketball jersey and drooping pants, parading across a stage in full view. I don't know who perpetrated this scheme, but they could not have had much insight into a kid's feelings.

In the end, I suppose it turned out alright. When

I became an older adult, instead of being called thin, people might remark, "You really keep in good shape!" as they contemplated their broadening waistlines.

There was a season when heavy clothes were a boon to my frame. In the winter, there in frigid Worcester, we needed plenty of protection as we waded out in the snow, which seemed to me at the time to be piled impossibly high, much higher than it ever accumulates now. Of course, when you are four or five feet tall, the perspective is quite different.

Winter is when the influence of the war was most evident in our clothes. I am speaking here about the years when I was between nine and twelve years old. There was a plentiful supply of military surplus clothing. It was cheap, and suited to the weather, at least to the standards of the time. That means we were swathed in some combination of wool and cotton, in outfits that were inevitably too big for us. I was given a white cotton parka to cover whatever else I had on. It must have been from some Mountain Division supplies. It featured an array of straps and cords and a large hood. It did seem to help against the freezing temperatures, but I always felt slightly embarrassed with this draped over me.

There were face masks too, of scratchy material, that had two eye holes and a place to admit some air into the nose. There were large gloves that extended halfway up the arm, and rubber boots with some sort of insulation that still required several layers of socks. No weather was too severe to keep us inside. This was an era in which fresh air was thought essential to maintaining health, so we tumbled around in the snow, well muffled by our military gear.

As far as grownups and their forties clothes are concerned, I have just a few, but clear recollections. One image comes from the day my family was walking to church on an Easter Sunday, when I was in the second grade. Catholic women, at that time, were expected to wear their hair covered when they entered a church. This extended to the times when a woman might be making a "visit" for a quick prayer, or running in to light a candle during the day, and she might not have a hat available. She would place a tissue or handkerchief over her hair to fulfill that edict.

Often, when attending Mass, a woman would wear a mantilla. This delicate veil might be worn by itself or attached to a hat. My mother seemed to always prefer that latter style. However, on this occasion, she wore a large, broad-brimmed straw hat topped by a large bunch of artificial fruit. There were grapes, apples, and pears, and perhaps other types as well. I thought she looked quite splendid.

One other point about dressing for church – my mother always wore white gloves. This practice led to an opportunity for a Christmas present for her – a new pair of gloves, presented in a flat box and wrapped with tissue paper. This would be prepared by the nice lady in the department store.

Men would not go off to work without donning a brimmed, felt hat with a creased crown. This was the classic fedora that Humphrey Bogart wore. My father had a grey as well as a brown hat. Both needed periodic shaping. This was called "blocking" a hat. I would hear a popular jingle on the radio, "I go for a man who wears an Adam hat." When Easter came, it was time for my father to don a straw hat. This was apparently cooler then the felt type. That transition applied to his suits. He was permitted by society to switch from wool to seersucker, a much lighter material.

When he wore a suit, often double breasted, my father would wear suspenders to hold up his pants. He referred to his suspenders as "galluses," an expression he probably got from his Irish father. Not only that, he would hold up his socks with garters – straps that cinched around his calves. Those suits, by the way, would always be worn with a white, starched shirt.

In wet or snowy weather, he would wear either rubbers – stretchy coverings for his leather shoes – or overshoes. These were high-topped rubber boots with metal clasps. The Irish influence led him to call these his "galoshes."

For her part, my mother wore a large, tight, elastic girdle under her clothing, complete with garters that held up her long nylon stockings. (I only knew that because she would wash her girdle and hang it out to dry on the line.) Those stockings had seams that held them together at the back of the leg. A woman would not be seen out in public with bare legs. "Are my seams straight?" was a perennial question.

THE THINGS WE CARRIED

Perhaps I can only speak for myself when it comes to this topic, but I am confident that these descriptions applied to my friends as well. So, let's imagine me at the age of eleven, heading out for the afternoon in midsummer. I only had to say to my mother, "I'm going out," and off I would go in one of several possible directions. Let's assume that I was heading up over Hendy's field to my friend Roger's house. That would mean that I would be passing through some woods, and when I got to Roger's we would be apt to go up past the cow pasture, and take a ramble through the swamp and forest up behind Tessier's cider mill and orchard.

I would probably have my jackknife, with its black imitation bone handle, and maybe even a small hatchet attached to my belt, inside a brown leather case, in case something needed to be chopped. There would be a few coins rattling in a pocket, and quite possibly my pea shooter and a cluster of dried peas.

I should add a bit more detail here about pea shooters. These were hollow tubes, about six or seven inches long, sized to accommodate the average pea, or small rock. I would buy a box of dried peas at Kaplan's to use as ammunition. We would shoot at just about everything. Unfortunately, this sometimes included passing cars. We once decided this might be fun, until we targeted a motorist who pulled over quickly and chased us until we outran him.

Running around with a mouthful of hard, dried peas was just asking for trouble, but our parents were probably not fully aware of our pea shooting adventures. Those shooters would be useful if we spotted some bull frogs or maybe a snake or two.

A pack of matches would be handy. I might have brought along my small, folded magnifying glass. This could be used to check out the details of a bug, or held just close enough to an ant so that the concentrated sunlight would fry it.

Perhaps most important on this kind of sojourn would be my slingshot. In those early postwar years, we could acquire a special kind of artificial rubber, red in color, that was ideal for slingshots. It had just the right amount of elasticity and snap. We would cut a y-shaped piece of wood from a sapling, and tie two strips of rubber onto the arms. A small rectangle of leather was attached to the strap ends, and there it was, a highly functional weapon. I was skillful enough with my slingshot to knock a squirrel off a tree branch. We showed little mercy to animals in those days. Carrying a slingshot required having a supply of suitable stones. You could not depend on finding the correct shape and size when they were needed, so they had to be added to one's pockets as a precaution.

Of course, my set of supplies to be carried depended on my plans. The fundamentals required that I have at least a handkerchief, some money, and my jackknife. If I were heading out to play curb ball I would need my small, very bouncy ball. If we were going to trade cards, or flip them, I would need a stack of baseball cards. Just for the fun of it, I might bring along my shiny Boy Scout whistle, the one with the wooden ball inside to make that special sound.

Although my pockets were often at capacity, I always seemed to be able to fit in whatever I might find – often in the street gutters. The gutters were a rich repository of stuff that people would drop there, back in those days before littering was considered an offense against the environment. We could usually find large pieces of cigarette butts, useful for gathering tobacco to sneak a smoke (more on that later). There was what seemed to be an almost inevitable find of coins, or sometimes an unsuspecting kid would throw away a popsicle stick with the word "free" stamped on it. This entitled the bearer to redeem it for a free popsicle!

Yes, I was well equipped for whatever might happen when I was wandering, when the only worry I might have is being sure I was home in time for supper. In the Fall months, that would be around the time that the street lights came on. Towards the end of the afternoon you could hear a chorus of mothers on the back porches, calling kids' names, in the hope that their missing children were within earshot.

GATES LANE

I have surprisingly few scenes that replay in my mind about my days at Gates Lane School, but those recollections that remain are vivid.

Entering the school, I would be met with a rich, unique aroma, a mingled atmosphere infused with the rich smells of crayons, colored pencils (we called them mongols), lunches of egg salad or peanut butter sandwiches hidden in desks, coats hanging in the cloak rooms situated in the rear of each classroom, wet galoshes and rubbers, and worn, oiled wooden floors.

Every classroom was furnished with a portrait of a stern George Washington, an American flag, and a large clock, whose swinging pendulum drove the black metal hands towards the next hour in audible ticks that resounded in the silent classroom. We sat in neat rows, at wooden desks fixed in place. Each desk top could be raised to store our books, lunches for those who did not walk home like I did, and other needed equipment. The latter included ink pens and a supply of small flannel patches – the pen wipes.

Writing in ink consisted in the following drill. Insert metal nib into wooden nib holder. Dip pen into ink well at right rear corner of desktop. Write until more ink needed. Dip again. When finished writing, wipe nib carefully with pen wipe.

We were given laborious handwriting lessons. The object of these drills was to instill in us the Palmer Method. That 19th century technique of cursive writing involves using the arm muscles to move the writing instrument rather than the fingers. In order to practice this, we used our ink pens to draw "ovals." These egg-shaped forms were to be linked from left to right, forming what looked something like a barbed wire fence, minus the barbs. To a left-handed kid like myself this was nearly impossible. I always made the worst ovals in the classroom.

It seemed quite natural for us to learn to write in cursive. After all, all handwriting had been done in that style for centuries. Printing was considered a lazy, careless act. Today, it seems, cursive training is becoming obsolete, thus turning those centuries of written records into the equivalent of a language foreign to young readers.

My third-grade classroom was ruled by Miss Healy. She was a tall, large woman who favored vivid shades of red lipstick, and had black hair styled in a Dutch cut. We were convinced that a male teacher, who periodically would come into the room to consult with Miss Healy in a whispered conversation, was romancing her. We thought that they might someday disappear together, but that never happened.

Unfortunately for us, she had traveled to Mexico in the previous summer, and had seemingly become obsessed with the culture South of the border. For a long time, she insisted that we come to school each day with a colored drawing on a Mexican theme. She would post the best efforts on the top border of the blackboards.

It did not take long before we began to run out of ideas. There were just so many versions of a Mexican dressed in a sombrero and a big hat while sitting under a cactus. Of course, we could always draw the castanets that Miss Healy had brought back, which she would shake while crooning a Spanish tune. I suppose she realized eventually that we needed to move on to another subject.

Something very important happened in the third grade. I skipped the second half and transitioned directly into fourth grade. This came about because I had started school in January rather than September, so I was always out of sync with the regular school year. By the time I was halfway through third grade, my parents decided that I should "catch up" with the kids that were ahead of me, and enter fourth grade.

The results were twofold. First, I ended up being the youngest kid in my class, and I missed the months of arithmetic when the students learned fractions. I would enter college at the tender age of 17, and have always struggled with those darn fractions. I think the former gave me the most trouble.

I see myself sitting at my desk in the fourth grade. I do not remember the teacher's name, but I cannot forget the following scene. *P* was a kid who lived not far from me. He had some kind of condition, mental or physical, that resulted in him wetting his pants. Because of this, in the Boy Scouts his nickname was "Stinky."

The heating system in the school was forced hot air. There were steel grates here and there in the floor for circulating the air. One of those grates was located just outside our classroom. One day, *P* did his thing. The teacher marched him out of the classroom and sat him in a chair placed directly over the grate, so that he would dry out. He was now on public display. Not only that, the odor of his wet pants wafted along the corridor. I remember his face as he sat there – as though he were in the stocks in the colonial era.

My sixth-grade class was taught by *Miss P*. Our classroom faced Main Street. Off in the distance, we could see a busy railroad line beyond a large, crowded lumber yard. (This place would burn not long afterwards, producing a memorable, spectacular conflagration.)

One day, we heard the whistle of a passing locomotive. *Miss P* stopped her lesson and said to one of the boys, "What train is that?" I do not remember his exact answer, but it was something like, "Oh, that's the 11:30 freight train heading south to New Haven." That is how we discovered that he knew all about train schedules. I had always figured him to be a smart kid because he was quiet, had sandy hair, and wore glasses. That performance clinched it.

The other student that I remember from that class is *D*. He was the fattest kid any of us had ever known. The desks we had were not designed to accommodate someone of his dimensions, nor were there any concessions made for his problem. However, *D* somehow managed to squeeze himself into the space behind his desk. He sat there off to my right, his ample behind hanging over the edges of his seat.

During the sixth grade, I was rewarded with an assignment that was reserved for the better students, or at least that is what I assumed. Periodically, the governor of the State of Massachusetts would sign a proclamation announcing that a certain day was dedicated to some notable cause or person. I was asked to read one of those proclamations in each classroom. This consisted in me entering a classroom, explaining to the teacher why I was there, and standing in the front of the classroom, where I would unroll the proclamation and read it aloud. The only words I remember are, "A proclamation by his honor, Governor Paul A. Dever."

Miss P was a short, dark-haired woman who used heavy doses of perfume. At the front of the room, next to the teacher's desk, there was an oak door that led into a small storage room. *Miss P* would often open that door and partially close it behind her. She would stand there peering into a mirror mounted on the back of the door, applying her makeup and lipstick. This unusual behavior became more frequent as time went by. One day, after emerging from the closet, *Miss P* walked past my desk. I could see tears in her eyes.

A few days later, the principal was present when we arrived for class. He told us that our teacher would not be back. We would have a substitute. I have always wondered whatever became of poor *Miss P*.

I do know what became of an earlier Gates Lane principal, Pop Andrews. He announced his retirement, and told the students that he planned on travelling "around the world." Sure enough, a year later he showed up and bored us with endless slides of his adventures.

WOODLAND PREP

I spent my seventh and eighth grade years at Woodland Prep. Because I was considered to have some academic promise, I was wrenched out of Gates Lane, and told to take a daily bus a few miles away to a new school that was designed to mimic high school. For the first time, I would be changing classrooms to cover different subjects. Each subject would be taught by a different teacher. No more sitting in one classroom all day listening to the same teacher. I would be studying Latin and French and algebra, and have a chance to learn some "practical arts" such as woodworking. That sounded good in theory, but the result of this move took me away from all the kids that I knew and played with, a separation that cost me dearly.

I will relate only a few of my experiences at Woodland Prep, because the Fall term of seventh grade marked the end of the 1940s, the era covered by these reminiscences. These two years marked the end of my childhood, my entrance into adolescence, and a new and utterly different decade. I retain a keepsake of those last months of the 40s in my right hand.

One day, after the end of recess, I was in a gaggle of students who were swarming up the stairs to the second floor. I must have bumped into the boy in front of me. It was *Jack*, a tough kid with short, wiry red hair and a mean reputation. He whirled around and gestured at me with a pencil held in his hand. I raised my right hand in defense, and he plunged the tip of his pencil into my palm. A small fragment of graphite broke off and lodged itself in my hand, where it remains to this day. The wound bled a bit, but never became infected or sore. However, the tangible proof of Jack's pencil attack never left me. You might say that he really got under my skin.

FRIENDS

Although I admit to have been something of a loner as a kid, I did have some friends. As I mentioned earlier, when you are a kid, the subject of friendship is complicated. There are categories of friendship, flexible to be sure, that define relationships. There are, for example, "best" friends, "good" friends, casual acquaintances, and kids you "know" but don't have anything to do with. Membership in these categories can shift overnight. A casual remark or an extra hard push in a touch football game can change a relationship in an instance.

The kids in my school and church were, with few exceptions, Irish-American Catholics. That is not an exaggeration because I can recall clearly the "different" ones. There was *Richard*, of German descent, *Ernie*, French Canadian, as was the chubby kid down the block, "Frenchy." Roger's father was from Finland. Arthur was the lone Jewish kid I knew. That's pretty much it.

I never saw, met, or spoke with an African-American until years later when I was in graduate school. I was aware that over on the opposite side of the city there was an Italian and a Polish "section," but that seemed OK because they were Catholic. Our side of the city was dominated by the Irish, as was the political life down in City Hall. As for Asians of any description, that was limited to knowing about my father's visits to a Chinese laundry. He was fond of telling the story of the Chinese owner saying to him, "Lee? My name Lee too!"

The kids I knew were named after saints. That was the unwritten rule. Thomas, James, John, Francis, William, Joseph, Peter, Robert, David, or Charles led the list. I was given the baptismal name Thomas Francis Xavier, thereby ensuring that I would be protected by not one but two holy men.

This was not an era of "sleepovers" or "playdates." After all, Worcester, the "Heart of the Commonwealth" of Massachusetts, is in the center of staid New England. I don't know how much geography or the Irish personality influenced my relationships, but I cannot recall any kid ever entering my house to play or eat with us. I would occasionally be admitted into a friend's three-decker apartment for a short while, but pretty much all my interaction with others was outdoors.

There was the one time that I ended up in *F*'s basement. He and a couple of other kids asked me to try out his new boxing gloves. It seemed like *F* was the toughest of the group, because he took on all challengers. When it was my turn, I put on the pair of brown, puffy gloves, relieved that they seemed pretty harmless. Within a few seconds, I was getting belted in the face. My interest in boxing ended then and there. *F* and I remained friends, however. One day, he and I were promised an intriguing site. His older brother was due to come home from the Army because he had contracted what they told us was Rocky Mountain spotted fever. When his brother got out of a car, *F* and I were very disappointed that his brother was not covered with red spots.

I regarded Roger as my best friend. This may have been

influenced by the fact that I was jealous of him. He seemed to have permission to do stuff that was forbidden to me, like having a BB gun. His parents were open and gregarious, and I felt comfortable in his house. We hung around with each other a lot because we shared a deep interest in the outdoors. We spent hours hiking through the woods.

My time with other friends revolved around the changes of season. There was a bunch of kids who circulated around within what I considered to be my "world," an area of probably two square miles. On a sunny, warm day, or even in the cold or wet, there would always be one or a few guys who would show up to play at something – basketball, baseball, stick ball, card-flipping, curb ball, or touch football.

How could I be bored? It was easy to find stuff to do – we were kids who could always find someone to play with, at least until we had to get home to eat. Our parents knew we were out there somewhere, with friends.

As I mentioned earlier, a major shift occurred in my relationships with friends when I transferred to Woodland Prep. After I had completed the sixth grade I was selected as one of the "smart kids" who were plucked out of a comfortable life at Gates Lane School. We had to take a bus back and forth from this "advanced" school where we would go through the seventh and eighth grades.

The change in distance was minor, but the disruption of my relationships with my peers was major. Rather than continuing to play on the school baseball team, for example, I was studying Latin and algebra in a school that didn't have any teams. In the complex, shifting world of kid's friendships, I was left on the outside, looking in.

GIRLFRIENDS

True love is not confined to the adult world. As a kid, I experienced two intense bouts of love, often called, insultingly, "puppy love." The first happened when I was in the third grade. The object of my fascination lived in a house just beyond Kaplan's grocery store. *Gail* was cute, with light brown hair that she wore in a braid. She had a slightly raspy voice that delighted me.

One day, my sister Rosemary and I were walking down Eureka Street with Gail. Rosemary was in the middle. She turned to Gail and said to her, "He likes you." Then she turned to me and said, "She likes you too." That was a moment of true fulfillment.

Not long after that, I was walking down Main Street past her house and met someone who told me that Gail had moved away to a town just outside Worcester. Somehow, she had neglected to say goodbye.

About ten years later, I boarded a bus in downtown Worcester, heading for home. I spotted Gail seated halfway back. I recognized her immediately. She was looking out the window. I walked past her and sat in the last row.

My other love was *Marilyn*. I met her when I was in the fifth grade – or was it the sixth? I was given an encouraging sign of her affection for me when we were watching a movie in school, seated side by side. She let me hold her handkerchief.

That was the game changer. I asked her to go to the movies the following Saturday. She agreed, and told me her address. It was a green three-decker down near Webster Square. On the fateful day, I walked down Main Street to pick her up. I was carrying a neat ring that I had gotten in a Cracker Jack box. I found the house, went up to the second story, and knocked. Her mother appeared on the other side of the screen door. When I asked for her daughter, she said, "Oh, she went to the movies with her friends."

I didn't bother to go to the movies that day. On the way home, I fished the ring out of my pocket and threw it into the gutter.

THE GAMES WE PLAYED

We had an impressive list of possibilities for play. After all, we certainly had no pressing reason to stay in the house. What could we do there, by ourselves? Certainly, if the weather was impossibly bad, there was reading to be done, either books or comic books, or maybe listening to the radio. However, the action was outside, somewhere, usually with kindred spirits. Those, by the way, did not include girls. I knew a few of those creatures, but they were never part of our varied activities. That would certainly have been memorable because girls, at least those not in our family, tended to be somewhat alien figures. (Except, of course, for the two special exceptions mentioned above.)

If there were outdoor adventures to be had, in any weather or season, it could sometimes start with a bike ride. I had managed to buy an old bike for five dollars, and tried to fix it up as best as I could. The only bikes available then had fat tires that required rubber tubes inside. There were no gears to shift, just a set of pedals and a brake on the back wheel that was operated by pushing back on a pedal.

I hauled my bike into our dingy cellar by carrying it through the backdoor and down the stairs through a door next to the kitchen table. Apparently, the building safety codes had not required cellars to have a second exit. By the way, our cellar was not dignified by referring to it as a "basement." It did have a cement floor, but a couple of bare light bulbs turned on by strings hanging from the ceiling revealed a dusty coal bin, an asbestos shrouded coal furnace, and an old wooden work bench.

I found a can containing some leftover paint, and after some sanding to roughen the surface, I gave my bike a coat of shiny red. Then, all I needed to do was take off the flat front tire, remove it from the rim, and pull out the leaky tube. I opened my puncture repair kit, rubbed some adhesive around the wound, and applied a square rubber patch. After this had dried, I reassembled the tire and inflated it with a hand air pump.

Having a bike, I was able to travel farther afield than the 2 miles or so that constituted my walkable territory. One hot summer day, I set off with a couple of kids on a bike hike over to Auburn, a neighboring town. One of those kids told us that we could get a haircut there for a quarter, and it would last us all summer.

I put some food into my Boy Scout backpack and filled my Boy Scout metal canteen, the one with the thin, brown cloth covering. I faithfully used this canteen even though it somehow gave the water an awful metallic taste. We set off down Grandview Avenue and arrived at Stafford Street. This was, to me, a somewhat mysterious thoroughfare. That road featured a steep incline known to the locals as "Dead Horse Hill." We figured any horse attempting to scale that hill would meet its maker.

This made the climb in our bikes seem quite perilous. Not wanting to meet a horse's fate, we periodically dismounted and walked the bikes. We finally reached our destination and waited our turn behind a bunch of other kids. The haircut turned out to be a "pineapple." That style was to be distinguished from a more typical "butch." The latter left one with a short, erect crown of hair that would retain that shape with the application of butch wax and a good brushing. The former cut simply shaved off all the hair on the head except for a thin, barely visible stubble. This look was guaranteed to last most of the summer.

The ride home was easy. We cruised downhill, stopping only to sit on a stone wall and eat our lunch. Speeding down the road, I could feel the new sensation of the wind against my scalp. I did not feel uneasy at all about my new look. I cannot say the same for my mother's reaction.

* * *

I was at home one day when I received a phone call. It was quite unusual for anyone to call me, so I was surprised to hear one of my fellow Boy Scouts breathlessly asking me for help. He claimed that one of our mutual friends had fallen off his bike near the Fish and Chip store, and he wanted me to get there right away. In retrospect, I don't know why he thought I could be of more help than professional assistance, but I went outside, hopped onto my waiting red bike, and headed down the hill towards the scene of the accident.

As I neared the site I could see my friend sprawled on the sidewalk, with his bike tipped over next to him. As I got nearer I could see a bright red pool of blood spreading from his head. I pulled up, dropped my bike and rushed to his aid. Suddenly I heard whoops of laughter from behind the corner of the building. A bunch of my friends ran out from hiding, while my injured friend sprang up, wiping traces of ketchup from his brow. They had fooled me completely.

The only thing I could do was grin and bear it. They never knew that I was embarrassed and ashamed that I had been made a fool of. I am sure that reaction was not their intent, but it remained the result that I am describing these decades later.

* * *

While many of our outdoor doings were dependent on the weather, and hence seasonal, basketball was an exception. This was perhaps the universal favorite activity, with baseball a close second. There were several popular sites for playing basketball, and almost always one could find kids there already in a pickup game, or waiting for one to form.

I was a pretty decent player, and it always gave me great pleasure to approach a game in progress, or as two teams were being formed, and hear someone say, "We've got Lee." Sometimes there might have been an ulterior motive that made me a favorite. One Christmas, when I was about eleven, I received the gift of a basketball net. Those places where we played, for example, Gates Lane schoolyard, featured basketball hoops whose original nets had long since worn away, leaving the bare metal rim. These were often good enough, but having an authentic string net was a great treat. When a ball went through the net, it slowed down enough so that it could be retrieved under the basket instead of caroming off at an angle, requiring a chase to retrieve it. It could be awkward to decide who should do the retrieving.

When I showed up with the precious net, someone bigger than me would hold me up long enough to hang the net on the hooks attached to the rim. When it was time for me to go home, I would have to retrieve it, not always a popular move because I might not always be the last to leave.

The schoolyard, by the way, was not paved at that time. It was packed dirt with a healthy complement of stones. If we happened to be using my ball – several kids would bring their own – its patch, or a stone in the wrong place, would cause the ball to bounce off to the side at an awkward angle. This could upset a dribble at a most inconvenient time.

These little problems were not a major consideration. We would play basketball in almost every conceivable weather condition. Perhaps the ultimate test was during the winter. When it snowed, one or more of us would show up at the schoolyard and shovel off the playing surface, usually up to the half court line. As long as we were moving around, the cold temperatures did not cause any great difficulty.

In those days, when we were running around the schoolyard, the National Basketball Association (NBA) was in its infancy. Still, we kids were very aware that one of its most famous players, Bob Cousy, was living just around the corner from Gates Lane. He and his wife lived in a house on the street across from Our Lady of the Angels church. Although the "Cooz" started his Celtics career in 1950, he was already a basketball idol in Worcester because he had starred at Holy Cross College there, leading his team to national prominence.

One night, as I lay in my bed with the radio turned just the right way so that I could pick up the game broadcast, I was listening to Holy Cross play in Madison Square Garden in New York City. I was thrilled when I heard the announcer, in a loud voice, describe the scene as Cousy dribbled down the court on a fast break and "bounced the ball behind his back," bewildering the defender, and then laid it in the basket.

This always represented to me a turning point in modern basketball, as the "Cooz" made a startling, unique move so common now as not to be noticed. Basketball then was a somewhat stodgy affair compared to today. There were no jump shots or three pointers, just two handed "set shots" and flat footed "push shots." There was also the hook shot, still occasionally seen today and my favorite move when I was out on the courts.

It seems strange, but it is true, we were convinced that Bob Cousy would drive by one day, see us shooting hoops in the schoolyard, park his car right there on Main Street, and join us to give us a few pointers. Needless to say, that never happened, but we never gave up that fantasy when we played at Gates Lane.

Sometimes I would head over to Grandview Ave to see if I could get into a pickup game halfway down that street. There was a hoop on a telephone pole there. That was the site of some good games, although we had to stop now and then to let a car pass by.

There was a kid who lived over there who was always ready for a game. He was a good player, but he was one of those kids who would rather take a shot than pass the ball. He earned the title we would give a kid like that. He was a "gun."

If we were playing there in the Fall, maybe with the air redolent with the delicious and unforgettable smell of leaves burning in the gutter nearby, we could easily notice the nearby street light go on, which signaled that it was time to head home before the maternal voices began their chorus.

In the downtown Boys Club, easily reachable by bus, there was a unique basketball court. It was referred to as the "Cage." This was a wooden walled enclosure where the baskets, without backboards, were attached directly to the wall on either end of the court. This presented a hazard for anyone going in for a layup, or finishing a fast break. One could easily run smack into that dark brown wall, made of narrow slats.

The Cage was the scene of one of my basketball triumphs and casualties. I was trying out for a team whose name I cannot remember, but this scene is frozen in time. There I was, in the corner of the court, far from the basket. I was wearing a white t-shirt and a red plaid bathing suit. I did not own real basketball shorts, but I figured the bathing suit would do, although I found that it did not contribute to any good impression I was trying to make. Hemmed in by a defender, I pivoted to my left and let loose with a graceful right-handed hook shot. The ball arced gracefully through the air, and swished through the net.

Instead of congratulations, the young guy supervising the tryouts yanked me out of the game immediately, and began reaming me out in front of my potential teammates. He could not understand why I would take such a crazy shot. He did not know of my long experience with the hook shot, from anywhere on the court, honed by hours of practice. I did not make that team.

That probably was for the best. I was reluctant to

spend much time at the Boy's Club, because that was considered a place favored by Protestants. As a kid, those people seemed quite alien to me.

* * *

Another site for basketball was a rather long walk to Hadwen Park. This was reached by heading down Eureka Street, then turning left on Stafford Street towards Webster Square. Turning right at the lumber yard, I would walk across the bridge that spanned the busy railroad tracks. That road led in a short distance to Hadwen Park, a place that remains in my mind as a dark and dangerous place. That sense of foreboding hit me every time I descended the hill that led into the park. That location certainly had plenty to recommend it – a baseball field, several basketball courts side by side, and a pretty good fishing site.

One other spot where we had some good games was at my friend Roger's house. He had a basket attached to a tree trunk in his side yard, next to the stone wall that marked the edge of the woods leading down to Hendy's Pond. One day, Roger told me that after watching us play a vigorous game of one on one, his father had said to him, referring to me, "That kid looks real athletic." The remark has stayed with me as one of the most impressive compliments I have ever received. For a long time after that experience, I felt that the short, somewhat tattered, tan jacket that I had worn that day gave me a certain flair. I felt like a cool kid whenever I wore it.

* * *

Baseball was a close second to basketball as a major preoccupation. I am writing here about playing the game, not watching it. While we were somewhat aware of the Major League drama going on at the time, we did not pay nearly as much attention to it as we might today. That probably had to do with the fact that we had only the radio to bring us the games, and that was generally limited to whenever the Red Sox were playing in Boston. I don't recall paying any special attention to the stars of the day – Ted Williams, Joe DiMaggio, Stan Musial, Bob Feller, or Jackie Robinson. The latter's groundbreaking entrance into professional baseball did not seem to have made any impression on me. (However, we were certainly enthusiastic about collecting baseball cards. More on that later.)

My baseball equipment consisted of a fielder's glove, a catcher's mitt, a bat, and several old baseballs. My father bought me my first baseball glove at Sears and Roebucks. This was a memorable adventure. We took the bus downtown, got off at the large, imposing store on Main Street, and headed to the sports department. We picked out a typical glove of the day – probably in 1945. When I got home, I began the process of preparing the orange glove for play. First, I rubbed the palm area of the glove with neatsfoot oil, and then placed a baseball in this area that would become the "pocket." I then wrapped the glove with heavy twine and let it sit for a couple of days. This process formed a more functional glove than its original flat shape.

I used that glove for years until I had to find a larger one for my growing hand. The source of my catcher's mitt is lost in the mists of memory. More than likely I found it abandoned somewhere. Most of our pickup games featured a jumbled pile of gloves and bats left near the first base line. Not everyone had a glove, so we would share whatever we had. Some kids owned bats which were ideal for their size and weight – but these too went in the pile.

If you were playing first base, you would need a special type of glove, and the same for catcher, so this system of sharing was crucial. Of course, if you were going to catch behind the plate, you would need to at least wear a mask. Any other protective gear was a luxury seldom acquired. If nobody showed up with a mask, the kid catching would play farther back from the plate to prevent getting a foul ball to the face.

I am guessing that I may have picked up a discarded catcher's mitt. It certainly had seen better days. I gave it new life, however, because I discovered that if I borrowed one of my mother's kitchen sponges and placed in inside the mitt, it cushioned the shock of catching a fast pitch.

My bat was given to me, probably for Christmas. It was a great bat until I, or a borrower, struck a ball low on the handle and the bat cracked. This required repair. I headed down to the cellar, found a hand drill, and made a pilot hole at the site of the fracture. Then I inserted a wood screw, tightened it up, and wrapped the area with black friction tape.

The bat was once again useful. However, I had to be careful to rotate it so that the force of the ball striking the bat would not put any additional pressure on the affected area. The wrong angle produced a shock that I could feel from my hands up to my shoulders. That bat was not often chosen from the pile of shared equipment.

Another challenge at our pickup games was the ball. I do not think I saw a new baseball – one of those beautiful, shiny ones that come in a box – until I was on the Gates Lane school team in the fifth grade. Usually, kids would contribute a yellowed, scuffed relic of a once pristine sphere. These worked perfectly well, although their dark shade made it tricky to follow if someone hit a ground ball.

We sometimes resorted to making our own. I once made a pretty decent ball using the following method. I took an old golf ball and laboriously wrapped it with heavy twine. When the ball wrapping reached baseball diameter, I wrapped it with white friction tape. Surprisingly, this reacted somewhat the same as a real ball, except that it took a mighty blow to hit that thing to the outfield. Eventually the tape split and that loose end started flapping in the breeze as it flew through the air. Still, it was fun.

Most of my baseball adventures took place at Bennett Field. That name brings back a scene still in sharp focus. I am walking out of my house at 1351 Main Street one morning in the spring, around 1947. The air has that hint of warmth that had been absent for so long during the long winter. The ground had recently thawed, and the delicious smell of wet earth on that balmy morning heightens my anticipation. I head down along Main Street towards Bennett Field, situated next to Gates Lane.

I am carrying my glove and bat, just knowing that there will be a bunch of kids at the field putting together a game. I get there, and somebody says, "We got Lee." And the game is on, the first of a new season with limitless hopes.

Standing at the plate at Bennett one could look out towards left field and see a cracked concrete wall about eight feet tall. Beyond the wall a steep hill rose towards a farm with a large horse barn. Looking towards right field, the school stood about 500 yards away, separated from the field by a patch of woods. Out behind center field lay the entrance to a path meandering away through a swampy area and up towards the woods leading to Coes Pond. Turning away from home plate revealed a view, across Main Street, of a scrubby wooded area of several acres extending over to Stafford Street.

This dusty field, with its patchy grass and pebbly infield, was the scene of many an adventure for me. Those included being a pitcher on the Gates Lane School baseball team during fifth and sixth grades. They gave us real uniforms and good equipment. In fact, when I approached the mound to begin pitching, the umpire would toss a perfectly white, smooth baseball to me. That ball felt magical. I could see its whiteness arc through the air as I threw my trademark looping curveball towards the batter. (Many years later, I attended my Holy Cross College reunion. During a game of golf that weekend, a guy that had gone to Gates Lane with me told our foursome, "Lee used to throw a great curve ball." He had been a witness to history.)

Every so often, I would look over at the sidelines or behind the screened backstop and spot my father. He would get off the bus on the way home from work to watch his spindly son play ball. That made me feel special. I always felt close to my father, but at a distance.

In one memorable game, I pitched so effectively that there were no hits against my tosses. In other words, I pitched a no-hitter! But alas, the circumstances of that game were most unfortunate. Our team was so powerful that we managed to score so many runs that the game ended after two innings. There was a rule that if a team was ahead by more than ten runs, the ump had to declare victory for the dominant team.

Even so, I anxiously scanned the newspapers the next morning, hoping that perhaps they would report my feat. That was not to be. I still feel that I was robbed of at least some praise.

Because I transferred from Gates Lane to Woodland Prep, where I attended the sixth and seventh grades, I lost out on the opportunity to continue playing on the baseball team, not to mention losing touch with most of the kids that I hung around with.

There I was one day, watching my former teammates in a tightly contested game at Bennett Field. *Dick* came tearing around third base, heading for home. The throw came in to the catcher, who stood on the third base line, blocking the plate. Dick slid hard, trying to knock the ball from the catcher's mitt. There was a loud snap, and the crowd suddenly became silent. I was close enough to see that a white bone was protruding from the runner's leg – a classic compound fracture. I can still hear that sound.

Speaking of baseball trauma takes me back to Maloney Field. This was a popular baseball field on Cambridge Street, about four miles from my house. In addition to the school team and numerous pickup games, I also played for a CYO (Catholic Youth Organization) team sponsored by Our Lady of the Angels church. This was great because they would hire a bus that would transport us around the city to face other CYO teams, pitting Catholics against each other. That did not seem unusual to me, considering that I knew only a small handful of kids that were not of that faith. (This plethora of Catholics led to some amusing headlines reporting school scores, e.g., "Saint Peter's Crushes Mary Magdalen".)

So, there we were, playing at Maloney Field. Although I did not know it at the time, my paternal grandfather, also a Thomas, who died before I came on the scene, had operated a small grocery store almost across the street from where we were playing.

This field was the scene of a flawed but satisfying baseball memory. I came up to bat. The pitch came in, and I took what I considered a mighty swing. The ball headed out toward left center. It was hit hard enough so that it managed to roll between the left and center fielders. Because grass was scarce out there, my hit rolled along the dirt surface and scooted through a hole in the bottom of the tall screen fence. I kept on running until I reached home plate. I discovered, to my relief, that this was regarded at Maloney as a home run.

I felt a surge of pride, and expected that my feat would elicit a chorus of praise from my teammates. That did not happen. That incident, along with my "no-hitter," made me feel that I was owed some applause. (Strange how often I remember feeling a need for approbation. I hope that didn't carry over to my later years.)

Maloney Field was the site of a tragedy that far over-shadowed any disappointment I ever experienced there. One day, *Tommy* was fooling around down by the railroad tracks that coursed along the field just beyond the first base line. Worcester was busy with train traffic, both passenger and commercial. A busy freight yard was not far from the field, and trains would often be slowly moving into position there.

Tommy decided to hop onto one of these railroad

cars as it slowly passed. These typically had a ladder attached to the side of the car, and kids would grab on and ride for a while, hopping off before the train would get to the yard. This time, Tommy slipped, fell off, and the train passed over his legs.

Traveling to Maloney Field or the Cambridge Street area in the years after that, one might see Tommy, rolling along slowly in his wheelchair, without the legs he had once used to skip up onto that massive train, just for fun.

* * *

It was not necessary to play baseball on a team, even if it was just a pickup team. We could play catch. It only took two kids, two gloves, and a ball. If a baseball was not available, we could use a tennis ball, or some other type of ball. We could spend a long time just throwing that ball back and forth, often across the width of the street.

I liked to play catch with my friend and neighbor Arthur. He lived across from me, on the opposite corner of Eureka Street, above his father's small grocery store. Behind the store there was a large yellow garage. (It had probably been a horse barn years earlier). I would lend my catcher's mitt to Arthur, a small, pudgy, dark skinned Jewish kid. He would stand in front of the garage and I would stand across the street, just about far enough away to simulate the distance between the pitcher's mound and home plate at Bennett Field. This gave me a chance to hone my pitching skills.

* * *

We didn't play as much "stick ball" as baseball. However, we had some great games about halfway down Henshaw

Street. There was a kid who lived there across the street from *Jerry*, the kid who beat me up one day in the schoolyard. I guess I should clear that one up before I get to stick ball games.

This kid Jerry was one of those tough kids who we might today characterize as a bully. He was the younger brother of *Eugene*, a kid in my class. I was in the fourth or fifth grade – a skinny kid with a mild temperament. I guess that made me a potential victim. One day at recess, out there in the dirt schoolyard, Jerry confronted me with a challenge to fight him. This confrontation quickly attracted a bunch of onlookers.

My reaction to him lives forever in my memory, and remains unresolved. I said to him, "My mother told me not to fight." This reply pleased neither Jerry nor the crowd, and he proceeded to knock me down and sit on top of me with a raised fist. I repeated my pacifist defense, and he gave up in disgust. Was I right to react that way? Should I have tried to fight him? My instinct then was to be a "good" boy.

Anyway, getting back to stick ball, playing down there on Henshaw Street always seemed to be a foray into an intriguing adventure. That's because the father of the kid who lived down there was some sort of politician who traveled to Boston to do his business, whatever that was. Somehow that fact gave the whole scene a kind of exotic feel. I used to think that I might even see his father, who I expected to look like a special kind of human.

I don't recall ever spotting him, but I did enjoy the games. They were pretty simple, really, just a broom handle for a bat and some kind of ball. If there were cars parked, we could use them for bases. There was little traffic, so we did not have to get out of the way often. After all, this was not exactly a New York City street.

One of the things I liked about those games was the fact that my friend Jimmy's big brother would play. At that age, around nine or ten, anyone who was eleven or twelve seemed awfully old and mature. To impress a kid like that left a warm glow of self-esteem.

* * *

Our interest in baseball led to another wildly popular pastime – baseball card flipping. This usually took place down at the corner of Henshaw Street, using the big brick wall behind Sal's drugstore – the one featuring a painted Coca-Cola ad on its surface. This was a little tricky, because the wall was on a descending hill, but we adapted.

The game required only a supply of baseball cards and a willingness to sacrifice some of them. We got the cards by buying packs of gum. Included with several flat pieces of pink bubble gum were cards, each featuring a picture of a professional baseball player, along with that player's statistics. The cards were treated as valuable collector's items. One's collection could be augmented by trading cards, often by exchanging ones which were "doubles," i.e., extra copies. Or, you might offer a couple of lesser players for a more prestigious one.

You might trade a Ted Williams for a Joe DiMaggio, or perhaps be willing to give up two Stan Musials for one Yogi Berra. I discover with amazement what would be the current value of some of the baseball card collections we stuffed into shoe boxes without ever regarding them as an "investment."

We would head down to Henshaw and challenge each other in a game of both dexterity and luck. Standing about six or seven feet away from the wall (behind a carefully monitored line drawn on the asphalt), one kid would throw a card toward the base of the wall. Then the other kid would toss a card towards the vicinity of the first card. Whichever card was closest to the wall was the winner, and the owner of the victorious card would pick up both.

Often, both cards would be touching the wall. This would be a "tie." The cards would remain there and there would be a new toss. Or, you might get a "leaner." The card would end up leaning against the wall. That would be a winner.

In this simple contest, our baseball card collections were built up and diminished while introducing us to powerful feelings of loss and gain. We were mercifully unaware of how those same emotions would enter our lives in the years to come.

* * *

Getting back to a more physical sport, another use for those tennis balls, often available although no one I knew ever played tennis, was for playing curb ball. We often used an even better ball, one of those pink rubber ones that could bounce really high. The curb along Henshaw Street near *Davy*'s three-decker was especially favorable for this sport. It had a nice sharp edge to it. If you stood in front of the curb and threw the ball at just the right angle, it would carom off that edge and fly across the street where the other kid was waiting. If he caught it, you were out. If the ball flew far enough, it might go over the hedge in front of Davy's. That was a home run, except for whenever the fielder would leap up and fall back into the bush, making a spectacular catch.

That took a real athletic effort, and resulted in some permanent alteration of the shape of the hedge. Usually, though, the angle of the original was not perfect, and the ball would run across the street along the pavement. If caught, it would be an out, and if missed, a single. Of course, the ball might bounce forward off the top of the curb, necessitating a trek into an empty lot to retrieve it. We favored Davy's site because of the hedges, but sometimes moved up the street a bit where an errant ball would merely fly up against the wall next to Sal's Drugstore and could easily be retrieved.

There was one complication that sometimes came up at that favorite site of our curb ball contests. Along the side of the street right in front of Davy's hedge was a sewer grate. These were sites designed to drain away rain water sluicing down along the gutter. Each of these grates was a heavy, perforated steel plate. There was a narrow opening against the curb, so that water could pour into the scary, dark depths of the drainage system. The ball could not get through the narrow slits of the grate, but it could escape into the opening at its rear, and be lost forever.

One day, searching for a glimpse of a fated ball floating on the black water about four feet below, we spotted something we never expected. There was a population of small frogs living down there! Where could they have come from? There they were, all blackened and slimy looking.

Of course, being kids, we invented ways to make the poor creatures lives even more miserable. If we dropped a small rock at the just the right spot through the grate we could bean a frog, to the poor animal's surprise. We even used the fishing pole trick for catching frogs in the pond. If we tied a small piece of red cloth onto a fishing hook, we could lower it through the grate and wiggle it in front of a frog's face. It would leap at the cloth, get hooked, and then we could pull it out. The frog's freedom was short lived, because it would be tossed back into his subterranean home.

Those sewers always stirred a feeling of fear in us. What if the grate gave way and we fell in? Would we be swept away into a foul, watery grave? I tried never to step on a grate. You just never knew.

* * *

The empty lot behind Morris' Market, situated beside Sal's drugstore, was the site of some great punch ball games. The lot was somewhat angled downward, so one had to run uphill to get from first to second. The setup was the same as a baseball game, except we pitched a large, black rubber ball with plenty of bounce to it. The batter would swing with one arm extended and hit the ball with a forearm.

A good blow could send the ball soaring up, hitting somewhere on the back side of a three-story apartment building, with each story having a large porch. If we were lucky, the ball would bounce back into the field of play. Otherwise, it might remain on a porch, or even worse, come in contact with a window. Whatever the case, when a fielder got hold of the ball he would attempt to throw the runner out by striking him with it. This would be accomplished simply by throwing the ball at him. The runner was out if struck. There were some pretty spectacular throws from the outfield that caught a kid running from third towards home.

* * *

Marbles became a favorite pastime for me and some of my friends in the mid 1940s. I amassed a hefty collection of marbles, those beautiful colored glass spheres. There are all sorts of names for various types of marbles, but we just described them as cat's eyes, aggies, or just plain. The latter were one color and clear throughout, or solid. The cat's eyes had this swirl of color radiating out from the center of the marble. Aggies were the bigger sized marbles.

I spent lots of time spreading out my marble collection on the floor and admiring their beauty. It's not that they were awfully valuable. They were relatively inexpensive. However, their beauty made giving them up all the more difficult. Those treasures did not have a long shelf life because we would compete for them in the neighborhood back yard dirt.

We only needed to dig a shallow, concave depression in the soil, move back about ten feet, kneel, and try to roll a marble into the hole. If you rolled one in, it would stay there until your second attempt, provided there was one. The next player would take a turn. If he managed to roll his marble into the hole, he would win whatever marbles were there.

So, marbles were won and lost. Sometimes I would return home with new marbles to add to my mesh bagful. Or I might be mourning the loss of some of my treasures. There were plenty of other marble games played all by myself in the strip of dirt behind my house. As with all the other treasured items that I collected as a kid, I try to remember just what became of them, but never can recall. Did I just put them aside as I got older? They seem to be still out there somewhere, just beyond reach.

* * *

Back in those days, professional football was nowhere near as popular as it is today. We were aware that such teams existed, but they could only be followed by reading a newspaper, which never seemed like a kid's business. However, there was a local college, Holy Cross, that generated lots of interest by us. Bob Cousy had turned the spotlight onto "The Cross" from 1945 to 1950 with his basketball exploits, and I enjoyed listening to their football games as well.

I invented a way to follow a football game on radio that went beyond just hearing it. I drew a rectangle representing the field on a large piece of paper. I added pencil lines for the gridiron look. Down on the living room floor, with the small radio turned at just the right angle to receive the action, I would indicate each play by drawing a line along the field the appropriate distance. With that scheme, I could plot the entire game and be left with a visual record of all those exciting plays. During the game, I would move a small button on the paper to represent the movement of the ball.

My friends and I loved to play football as a pickup sport, usually in an empty lot near my house, or on the pavement down on Henshaw Street. This was touch football, the game in which a kid's progress could be halted, not by a tackle, but simply a touch.

Like our basketball or baseball adventures, any specific football game depended on somebody contributing a football. My favorite ones were the smaller ones that I could grab hold of. I am reminded of two football triumphs that ended as these feats usually did for me.

The first happened in seventh grade. We were playing a quick game in the stony school yard at Woodland Prep. The football was a small, soft, yellow ball with a suede-like leather exterior. I was playing defense at the climactic moment. As *Donald* faded back to pass, I rushed towards him and raised my arms as he threw the ball. I blocked his throw, and the ball flew straight up and behind him. I continued to run toward the ball, grabbed it, and ran to the goal, scoring a touchdown.

At that moment, the bell rang. We immediately began filing back into school. I looked about, waiting for the congratulations that I expected would be heaped on me for what I felt was an exceptional athletic feat. No one said a word to me. Not then, not later. Didn't any one of them know what I had accomplished?

My second triumph took place in the only football game I can recall played in Hendy's field, directly across the street from my house. There were a bunch of older kids in that one, but I managed to get in on the action. This time it was tackle football, a pretty rough choice considering all the acorns that were lying around, having dropped off the giant oak tree looming over the field of play.

There I was on that day, waiting to receive a kickoff if it should come my way. It did just that, and I gathered it in. I headed down the field, my teammates blocking the defenders. One kid stood in my way. He lunged toward me, bending down toward my legs, ready to tackle me. Without hesitation, I leaped into the air and jumped right over him, and scampered across the goal line.

The game continued as though nothing had happened. What were these guys thinking? Weren't they supposed to gather around me, clapping me on the back and expressing their astonishment at what I had just done? Right over the guy! (There I go again.)

Well, maybe one of them is writing his memoirs now, and remembers that cool Fall day when that kid, whatever his name was, made a great play. Perhaps he is the very kid I jumped over. Just maybe.

* * *

Then there were horseshoes. This was not a sport that most of my friends played. However, there were two sites where I became adept at throwing those heavy shoes into a sand pit that had an iron rod sticking up in the middle, serving as a target. My friend Roger, who seemed to have pretty much anything a kid might want, had a horseshoe setup in his side yard.

He got the best of me in pretty much everything, but I managed to keep up when it came to horseshoes. I developed a technique that involved grasping the shoe on one side and throwing it so that it turned, not end over end, but in a flat, slow spin. If done just right, the shoe would make one slow revolution, tip slightly downward, and its open end would meet the post with a clang. What a sweet feeling.

I also learned to catch a horseshoe thrown by my opponent. Of course, this was only a demonstration and not part of the game. I discovered that the trick was simple – just reach out and as the shoe went by, grab it and move my arm in the same direction as the shoe was moving, and then pull it down around my back. As a kid, it helped to be able to do at least one cool thing.

The other horseshoe site was on Stafford Street, at the far end of Eureka Street. There was a diner across the street from that intersection. The owner was a friendly guy who let us use his horseshoes whenever we showed up. In fact, he would come out sometimes in his white apron and toss a couple of ringers as a demonstration of his artistry.

When I played there, my opponent would be S He was a young man who would now perhaps be labelled as a "special person." His limited talents certainly extended to an ability to play horseshoes, and we had some spirited contests down there next to the diner. The latter, by the way, was located not far from a relatively small building where it was rumored the owner had become quite wealthy during the war by manufacturing bandages there. I would learn later that the stories were true. The owner's home was located near my house, and included an apple orchard we would sometimes pass through, heading up to adventures in the woods.

* * *

During the winters, which seem to me now to have been much colder and snowier back then, when late December rolled around it was time to play hockey. The ponds were frozen solid, with ice thick enough to support a bunch of kids. If it had snowed, we would show up at Wooded's Pond, up around the corner from Hendy's field, armed with shovels. We would clear a large patch out in the middle, trying to steer clear of the northern edge of the pond, which was the site of a constantly bubbling spring. The ice would be thin there, and clear. If a puck happened to find itself racing towards that area it might slip through an opening and lie there, visible through the thin ice. It would take a careful approach to retrieve it, as well as someone willing to get their feet wet. The errant puck would be too valuable to abandon.

Because the hockey season usually started after Christmas, some lucky kids might be outfitted with new skates and sticks. The skates in that era were stiff leather boots that came with blades that needed careful sharpening. We did that with a contraption that consisted of a grindstone held in a clip. The blade was placed in the clip and rubbed against the stone to give it some level of sharpness. That was good enough for us, not knowing any other way to make the skates usable.

There were usually enough kids for a pickup game. We used two boots, separated by about three feet, for each goal. Our sticks would be wound with white hockey tape, taking care to put a knob of tape at the upper end to help keep a grip. Nothing worse than dropping a stick during a game.

There was a clear distinction between two groups of kids during these hockey games. Everybody who showed up could at least stand up on his skates (no girls were ever involved), but there were a few who could skate backwards. That is a skill not easily acquired. I was one of the unfortunates who were forced to make a laborious turn if I had to go in the opposite direction. This allowed kids like Roger, who not only seemed to have everything but could do everything as well, to swoop around the ice with grace, while most of us weaved around like drunken sailors. Still, it was great fun, and we could always take a break next to the fire that someone would light on the shore.

For some reason, we never used Hendy's for skating, just Wooded's. Last year I drove by the scene of those long-ago hockey games. The view of the pond was hidden by a couple of houses and some tall trees which seem to have grown up along the shore. There were no kids around.

* * *

While there were plenty of games to be played with a bunch of other kids, we enjoyed additional activities on our own. One popular one was fooling around with a yo-yo. Around the age of ten or eleven I had a treasured yo-yo, a black wooden one with an embedded "diamond." I could make it "sleep" or "walk the dog" or even go "around the world." Of course, just like with skating, there were kids with different skill levels using yo-yos. During recess, the schoolyard would be busy with kids spinning their yo-yos, with an eye to showing what they could do.

Another often solitary activity was bows and arrows. I made my own bow, but my parents did buy me some real arrows. To make a bow, you find a sapling of the right thickness and cut off a length of about three feet with your trusty Scout hunting knife. Peel off the bark, cut a notch at either end, and connect the ends with strong twine, while bending the sapling into the shape of a bow. Let that dry out for a few days and you have a serviceable bow. Arrows need to be perfectly straight, so my attempts at making my own were inadequate.

A bus trip to Sears and Roebuck with my father

yielded three wooden arrows, each with three orange feathers and metal tips. These worked beautifully, although I now realize that they could have become lethal weapons if launched in the wrong direction.

That almost became a reality one day when I set up a target on our side lawn. Standing across Eureka Street, I aimed an arrow at the target. The arrow flew over the target and headed straight for the house. I can see that arrow plunging into and through the living room window, leaving a neat hole. It turned out that my grandmother Nana was sitting by that very window. The arrow flew right by her. I have no recollection as to what happened to me as a result of that errant shot. Perhaps I am suppressing the details of the aftermath.

I did not confine archery to my yard. I would roam up along Hendy's and the nearby woods, taking shots at whatever looked interesting. In keeping with my usual indifference to animal welfare, bullfrogs, squirrels, and even birds were not spared as targets, although I can recall nailing only one hapless frog. Eventually my escapades led to the loss of those beautiful orange-tipped arrows. I don't believe they were replaced.

* * *

Another weapon that was common among my friends in those days was the BB gun. There was no way my parents would ever let me have one of those, but among my more liberated friends it was not unusual to receive one for Christmas or a birthday – usually the popular Red Ryder model.

As usual, my friend Roger had one. We would load up his gun with a bunch of BBs and go "plinking."

That is what we called shooting at whatever struck our fancy – a can, a bottle, or maybe a frog or squirrel. It took some skill to hit a target more than a few yards away, because the BB would quickly begin to drop after being propelled from the gun barrel by means of a spring mechanism.

While I sometimes had the opportunity to shoot a BB gun, I was also on the receiving end a few memorable times. Once, when I was walking along Main Street between Henshaw and Eureka Streets, a gun wielding kid was stationed down behind a three-decker, taking pot shots at vulnerable targets. He got me in the right leg on the run. It was quite an admirable shot that stung only a little.

One other incident was more painful. Across the street from my house was a short lane leading away from Main Street. At the end of this stretch there was a wooded area where some bigger kids had built a camp. This consisted of an underground chamber covered with branches and leaves to disguise the hiding place below. As I passed by one day, the campers burst out and grabbed me. One of them pinned my arms behind my back. Another pressed the business end of his BB gun onto the top of my sneakered foot and pulled the trigger. That one really hurt.

The BB gun incident that stands out as a crystal-clear memory is the following. One sunny summer day, I was standing on the shore of Hendy's Pond, casting my fishing lure. Walking down from the woods carrying his BB gun came *Tommy*, the very same kid that I had saved when he accidentally lit his altar boy surplice on a votive candle. He confronted me, and said that he was going to "pants me."

That specific torment involved grabbing a kid, pulling off his pants, and running away with them, leaving the kid in his underwear, wondering how he would get home half-dressed. That had already happened to me once before. A couple of kids had not only taken my pants, they had tied me to a tree up near the top of Hendy's field. Fortunately, the ropes were loose, and I was able to extricate myself. Then I sneaked down towards my house through the woods, and managed to run across Main Street without too many observers.

The thought of another pantsing motivated me to start running in the general direction of home. I heard Tommy hustling behind me, and as I turned and looked over my shoulder, he got off a shot that hit me squarely between the eyes. I stopped, and felt warm blood trickling down the bridge of my nose. I am sure that Tommy was more scared than I was at what he had done.

He took off as fast as he could run, and I headed up the hill towards Roger's house. I didn't dare to go home. Roger's mother kindly cleaned me up and put a small bandage on the wound. When I finally arrived home my mother was understandably upset. She phoned Tommy's mother and related what her errant son had done.

Tommy never gave me a hard time again. I have often thought of how different the outcome might have been had that BB landed a bit to the left or right, into one of my eyes. As for Tommy, years later I heard that he had become a policeman.

* * *

Another activity that would play an important role in my life as an adult had its beginnings for me in the late

1940s. It is not clear to me exactly how a handful of golf clubs came into my possession. I am pretty sure they had been lying around up in the attic – but these were my introduction to the wonderful world of golf.

Across Main Street lay Hendy's field, a broad, rising hill, separated down the middle by a row of trees – oaks, maples and birches. Looking across the street from my front yard, I could see, off to my right, on the lower corner of the field, a flattened area measuring about 50 yards from the street edge back to the woods. That became my golf hole.

I cleared a patch of grass about five by five feet near the woods, smoothed the dirt surface, and dug a hole to accept a soup can so that its top was level with the surface. This gave me a green and a cup. At the other end of this grassy strip I scraped an area to serve as my tee box. I had to cut away the tall grass between the tee and green so that I had a reasonable fairway.

My clubs had wooden shafts and smooth leather grips. Even then these would have been considered old fashioned equipment, but they served me quite nicely for the purpose. I had a "spoon," known today as a three wood, a "mashie," or five iron, a "niblick," a nine iron, and a putter. I don't know how I got hold of golf balls – they certainly weren't new – but armed with clubs and balls, I had all I needed. I learned to put a ball on a tuft of grass and hit it towards an area where it would bounce its way through the rough fairway, arrive at the green, and sometimes even go into the hole.

As I became more proficient, I realized that I could expand my horizons and construct a "real" golf course at Hendy's. I don't recall exactly how many holes I made, but I am sure it was at least five. They stretched from the top of the hill to the bottom, and across the width of the field. Now I could use all my clubs and swing as hard as I wanted. I see myself now, at the very top of the hill, ready to tee off, hoping that my mother could see me from the front door across the street.

Some years later, my father would present me with full set of used golf clubs. This time the clubs had steel shafts, but in keeping with the transition in the golf world from wood to steel, the shafts on these clubs were made to look like wood. They were MacGregor "Ben Hogan" clubs, long since lost to time and a vigorous garage cleaning. Another eBay treasure unrealized.

The hill featuring my golf course, always played alone, was the site during the winter where dozens of kids gathered to ski. It was the perfect spot for beginners – not too steep or too long. If you trudged up along the strip of trees in the middle of the field, taking care not to step on the trail that had been fashioned by the skiers, you could start at the crest and ski either to the left or right. If you went to the right, you could swoop down a broad expanse and arrive at the bottom with a flourish. You would quickly bring your ski tips together while keeping the tails apart, forming a "Vee" shape. A lean to the left or right would allow one ski to slide deftly around, paralleling the other. This move, assuming you leaned back a bit, would bring you to a stop, thus completing a "stem christie."

This maneuver, long since replaced by the parallel skiing method enabled by far superior equipment, was the accepted mode of stopping. In theory, it was simple, but it required entering the bottom of the slope at a sufficient speed to create the momentum allowing that graceful turn. Many a kid, including myself, would slow down a bit too much, and instead of swooping around in a flourish, would just stop halfway through the maneuver and fall down.

I can remember the acute embarrassment of making that awkward mistake in front of an audience. Some of them I knew, and others were strangers. That mistake required another trudge up the hill and a resolve to do it right. Eventually I learned to perfect the christie. This helped when I chose to make a left turn at the hilltop and ski down the steeper slope that ended on my first golf hole, now buried under the snow. The kids who chose the left side were the equivalent of today's skiers who head out on the black diamond trail. Come down that hill at breakneck speed and swoop into a finish complete with snow flying up off your skis at the end – that was a glorious moment.

The equipment we used added to the challenge. The skis at that time were long, wooden, heavy things whose bottom surfaces required careful, repeated waxing with a block of paraffin. Heavy, square toed boots were placed into metal bindings that held the boots by a spring mechanism. Theoretically, if you fell while skiing, this spring would snap open, releasing the boot from the binding, preventing ankle injury. A long leather strap connected the skis to the legs, so that the skis would not escape down the slope. The system worked well enough. However, after a fall leaving you in deep snow on a hill, resetting those bindings could be a major challenge.

This was not an era of Gore-Tex. Our ski clothes were supplied from the abundance of military surplus materials.

We had wool and cotton to choose from. My early ski outfit was topped by that absurdly large, white cotton parka designed for the Army's Mountain Division. It was topped by a large hood to pull up over my wool knit hat. The whole thing hung down almost to my knees.

Despite the impediments, I spent many happy hours on that hill, stopping only when my feet became too numb to feel. I would unbuckle my skis, put them over my shoulder along with my long bamboo poles with the leather netting at the base, and walk across the street to my house. I would leave my stuff in the back porch, enter the kitchen, and say to my mother, "Did you see me? Did you see me?" She would assure me that she had been watching, and that I was a good skier. I always expected my mother to be in the kitchen, and she always was.

* * *

In the late 1940s, a brand new recreational facility opened in Webster Square. Up until then, we were quite content with roller skating along the neighborhood sidewalks using the simple skates that clamped onto the sides of our shoe soles. These were metal devices that were adjustable, so that one pair was sufficient to keep a kid skating for years. There was a "key" that you wore around your neck on a cord. That little gadget was used to tighten and loosen the skates.

These skates, with their coarse metal wheels, were enough to give us hours of fun, as long as we learned how to traverse the cracks in the sidewalk and didn't go so fast that we were out of control. There wasn't a convenient way to stop once you were underway. By the way, those sidewalk "cracks" are the grooves formed where each section of the cement walk meets the next. They were the spots you never stepped on, following the warning, "Step on a crack and you break your mother's back." We always avoided them, just in case.

This new facility in Webster Square lent a new definition to roller skating. A large, renovated building supporting a prominent marquee announced itself as the "Skaterina." Inside was a large, oval, wooden floor, surrounded by viewing areas – mainly for cautious parents. It was basically like a hockey rink without the ice. There were neon lights, skates for rent – real ones with high leather tops – and refreshments. To top it all off, as the skaters glided, or lumbered, or stumbled along the wooden oval, there was live organ music in the background. It was an exciting, circus-like atmosphere.

The skaters would move in a counterclockwise direction for a while, and then be asked to reverse and go the other way. The clockwise direction is typically tougher to accomplish, so that this system led to some interesting traffic jams. In addition, the organist would change the tempo of the music now and then – moving from a slow, dreamy cadence to a waltz, and then a galloping rhythm. This would result in a few skaters toppling over. I can attest to the fact that falling on a wooden floor while roller skating is memorable.

Then there was always the show off kid – the one with a higher skill level, who would race by everyone, weaving in and out of the average kids – like me.

* * *

Busy Webster Square offered yet another possibility for athletic activity. Back in the late 19th century, a bowling alley proprietor in Worcester invented a radically different way to bowl. Up until then, a large, three-holed ball was used to attempt to knock down ten "pins." These pins are squat, wooden targets, each with a slender neck and a bulbous base. The bowler was given two chances for each of the ten "frames."

The new method of bowling introduced a smaller, solid ball, and wooden pins that resembled tall candles. There were three chances per frame. If a pin was knocked over it was allowed to remain there as "dead wood," and could be struck by a ball so as to sweep away the standing pins. Ever since this departure from tradition entered the world of bowling, the controversy over which form of the sport is superior has continued, and candlepin bowling is still pretty much confined to New England. For me, living in Worcester, known as the "Heart of the Commonwealth" of Massachusetts, candlepins was considered the true bowling religion.

Just off Webster Square, on Park Avenue, Metro Bowl was the nearest bowling alley. There were several more downtown where I would bowl when I was in high school and college, but Metro Bowl was just a long walk down Main Street.

Once inside the large, low white building one was enveloped in the heady aroma of waxed, wooden alleys, old leather bowling shoes for rent with the size displayed in big letters on the back of the heel, thick, black, wax scoring crayons, the buttery odor of machine-made popcorn, and the tang of the inevitable cigarette smoke.

The automatic pin setter was invented in 1947, when I was nine years old. It took years for this system to spread, so Metro Bowl offered a great chance for a kid to have part-time employment as a "pinboy." A young boy would perch just out of sight up on the edge of the area where the pins stood. After the bowler had either knocked down all the pins, or used up his or her three chances, the pin boy would jump down, pick up the scattered pins, and place them back in the assigned spots. Those locations were indicated by circles painted on the alley floor. He also picked up the balls and placed them on the wooden groove that would, simply by gravity, let the balls roll back to the bowler.

The kid would hop back up to his perch, ready for another volley. I had a friend who worked as a pinboy. Once, I wandered back to the busy, noisy end of the alleys to see the action. My friend motioned me over and asked if I wanted to give him a break and set pins for a while. Of course, I agreed, and took his place. Wow! I was not prepared for the fact that the flying pins were bounced around so forcefully that my legs were under attack. I had to keep track of how many balls had been thrown, and when it was time to set the pins, I was not exactly deft enough to quickly place them right onto their ordered rows.

I appreciated the experience, but was no longer fascinated by the thought of someday being one of those nimble pinboys.

* * *

There were indoor games as well, although I remember the outdoor adventures in more detail. These games often involved my parents and sister Rosemary. I retain a crystal clear recollection of the faces of the writers featured in the card game "Authors." This game used a deck of cards, each bearing a colored illustration of a famous writer along with his or her brief biography. The idea was to get a set of four of each by blindly drawing from another player's hand.

I would recognize each of those illustrations if I saw them today. There was the mustachioed Mark Twain, the blond, handsome Nathaniel Hawthorne, the dark-haired Edgar Allen Poe, and the bearded Henry Wadsworth Longfellow, as well as the prim Louisa May Alcott, the dashing Robert Louis Stevenson and an avuncular Charles Dickens. All in all, there were 13 writers whose works were in the canon of books to be read by kids, teens, and adults of the day.

Beyond that, I remember checker boards, and Chinese checker boards loaded for play with marbles. I would enjoy the challenge of a game of Pick-up Sticks. A collection of variously colored, slim wooden sticks, about seven or eight inches long and pointed at each end, would be dumped onto the floor. This would create a jumble of overlapping sticks. The goal was to remove sticks from the pile without moving any other stick.

This game required a high level of dexterity. Also, the players had to detect slight movements of sticks that might have been disturbed by the opponent. My clearest recollections of those games involve cries of "It moved!," "It did not!," "It did, I saw it!"

A more peaceful game, almost always solitary, was dominoes. I know now that this can be a somewhat complicated contest, but my interest was merely to line up those black, rectangular tiles in long rows and topple the first in line. The rest would fall, one after the other. The length of these rows would be limited by the number of tiles available. I would create complex patterns of dominoes, and call my mother in to watch as I tipped the lead tile. She would dutifully express her astonishment at what I had accomplished.

WOODED'S AND BEYOND

So far in this narrative, I have only hinted at the major preoccupation in my young life during those early years in Worcester. Between 1945 and 1950, when I was not in school, or playing some sport or game, usually out-doors, I would be "in the woods."

I lived on the edge of a large wooded tract that, to my imagination, stretched out indefinitely, perhaps all the way to Canada. The fringe of forest that was within my reach became my favorite haunt. I might be alone, or sometimes accompanied by my friend Roger and his small black dog Skippy. There was no point to my explorations beyond sheer curiosity, fed by the delicious belief that something interesting might be just beyond the next clump of trees, or under a pile of brambles, or maybe just over the next hill.

Here is a typical scenario. Telling my mother, "I'm going up to the woods," I would cross Main Street, walk up past the Henderson sisters' house at the bottom of Apricot Street, and turn right onto Wildwood Avenue. Then I would amble along that road where there were only a few houses, including that of the farmer who owned the cow pasture behind Hendy's Pond, which lay in a hollow just to the right of the road.

Sometimes, I might stop off at Hendy's and grab hold of the raft we had moored near the pasture, and go for a cruise. Roger and I had built this with logs we had gathered in the nearby woods, lashing it together with ropes. A long pole served to propel the raft across the pond. I am sure I never told my parents about this.

Moving on past Hendy's, I would soon reach Wooded's pond, the site of those spirited winter hockey games. I would cross the narrow field fronting Wooded's and skirt the pond along its right side, the spot where the spring bubbled up. That required a leap across a wet patch and a climb up towards the stone wall paralleling the water. I once saw a bobcat hopping along that wall, a sighting never to be repeated.

Over the wall, a faint path along the edge of a pasture led up over a steep hill to where Tessier's apple orchard spread out down along a hill to the left. From there, the path continued downward to the right, passing a bramble patch where I could usually depend on seeing at least one rabbit skipping back inside for safety. A tall, gray tree stood there, where I once saw a family of raccoons peering out from a large hole about twenty feet up on the trunk.

The path entered the woods where the noise of my approach might sometimes flush a pheasant up out of the underbrush. I might turn off to my right and walk down through some dense trees and bushes to a small, oval pond, only about 50 yards wide, lying in a hollow. I preferred to be with someone else when I visited that site. We all believed that this pond had no bottom. Once, I was with a bunch of kids who dared each other to go for a swim. To their surprise, I joined in, and did my bit of fake swimming across and back the width of the pond.

When I hauled out of the water, I became an instant hero, because there was a large bloodsucker attached to my leg. Applying my Boy Scout learning, I took out my jackknife and peeled that thing off my leg, and tossed it back into the pond. I was applauded for that cool act of courage. That incident added to the local legend – the pond was not only bottomless; it was teeming with leeches.

Usually I would head off to the left and thread my way down to the "Res." This was a small, abandoned reservoir, about 150 yards long. There was a column of stones in the center, standing about 15 feet high. The entire bowl of the reservoir was made from granite blocks. What had probably been a pump house sat on one end, where whatever rainwater that might collect would trickle out into an underground pipe.

A creek ran from a nearby swamp down along the woods about 20 feet from the far side of the Res. This proximity led to a scheme that became a legendary project. I was in on the idea which went like this. We – I do not remember the names of the others besides Roger – conceived the idea that if we could block most of the drainage from the Res, and dig a ditch from the creek, that would divert the water. It would fill up the Res, and we would have a grand swimming hole.

What sounds like a lamebrained scheme turned out to be workable. We jammed the drain, dug a ditch, dammed the creek, and watched the slow transformation of the Res from an empty hole to a brimming body of water. Apparently, there was enough drainage to allow sufficient water to leak out so that the water level remained rather constant.

I must add that this adventure was not beneficial for me. I had not learned to swim, whether at Boy Scout camp or in the YMCA. I will never forget the ignominy of the day the instructor hauled me out of the pool with a long hook, as my friends swam by me during beginner's lessons. Now that we had a popular swimming hole, I could only survive in the water through a combination of using a side stroke, dog paddle and treading in place. That led to some anxious moments as we all jumped in and headed for that column about 100 feet away.

* * *

Getting back to my sojourn, hiking past the Res brought me to the swamp. This was a great place for discovering birds, frogs, snakes, and turtles. Further on, a lengthy path through tall ferns led on to a large reservoir, where Roger and I would have some great fishing adventures. This town water supply was overseen by a caretaker who lived on the shore.

On an evening fishing trip, we would studiously avoid walking near the caretaker's house. We would sneak through the woods to get to the opposite shoreline, reasoning that when he spotted us, as he inevitably did, it would take the maximum time for him to get to us, allowing us time to escape.

That place was full of big bass, and we had our best fishing adventures ever, before we had to haul out of there and head for home. I had great luck with my Wobblehead lure armed with two treble hooks. I would cast that thing out and slowly reel it in, watching it wobbling and splashing along the surface. It was my favorite lure along with my Daredevil and Al's Goldfish.

Traveling beyond this reservoir seemed to be going

a bit too far, as though I would have entered a kind of wilderness. However, If I were to turn right on my way to that fishing haven, a trek through the woods would bring me to a very steep hill, topped by a flat plateau. I had to be careful when I mounted that hill, because I might be met suddenly with the view of a plane taking off just above my head.

This was the Worcester airport. Commercial and private planes flew in and out of that field, although certainly not with the frequency of today. They apparently did not have much security, because I would roam around the edges of the field and visit the small terminal without drawing any attention. Once, I was in the terminal with a friend who was wearing an Army surplus backpack. We put a coin into the popcorn machine. To our delight, the delivery chute stuck open, and the popcorn flooded out. We quickly opened the backpack and gathered a harvest for our hike home.

* * *

When I had gained some skill with my slingshot, Roger and I would head up past Wooded's to a spot where there were lots of oak trees. There would always be plenty of squirrels clambering around the tree trunks. A squirrel will scramble to the hidden side of the trunk if it spots an intruder. We would stand on opposite sides, giving one of us a look at the squirrel, and proceed to sling stones at it until we knocked it off to the ground. Roger's dog would then grab it, shake it, and finish off the job. Sometimes we would leave a few victims on the farmer's back porch. He had told Roger that they made a good meal.

* * *

One short detour on the way to the woods beyond Wooded's became another adventure. Heading off to the left, after scrambling over the stone wall, a short climb up through a stand of oak trees would bring me to the brink of a steep incline. It led down to a patch of water that collected between where I stood and the steep hill beyond.

A few friends, whose names are lost in the mists of memory, were with me one day as we explored that neck of the woods. We discovered a narrow path on the far side of the water. Walking single file along the trail, we decided that this area would now be known as "Two Pond Valley." It seemed like a perfect spot for meeting secretly, far from prying eyes. We then were inspired to fashion a hidden cache of supplies that we might need in case of emergency.

The next time we met there we were prepared with the required materials. Using out trusty Boy Scout Army surplus shovels, the khaki ones that folded up for easier carrying, we dug a hole. Into it we put a wooden box. Into the box we placed a length of rope, a flashlight, a whistle, a slingshot, a cap gun and a roll of those small, red caps, and various other items – things you just might need if you met with some sort of crisis up in the woods. If you were really in trouble, the whistle could warn your buddies that you needed help up there in Two Pond Valley.

We covered the box with a wooden lid, followed by leaves and branches, and notched a nearby tree as a marker. I remember going back there just once to check on the contents. They were there, just waiting for that emergency. Perhaps they are waiting still.

* * *

My trips to Wooded's included one regrettable incident. I was heading back home one mild Spring day, the kind of day when the Earth is awakening and the sun is gaining strength. On the grassy slope, directly in front of the Henderson sisters' house, a small spring had formed, and water was slowly flowing down towards the base of a large maple tree. As I passed the tree, I spotted a movement, a quick flash of green near the tree. As I watched, a snake about five or six inches long slithered out of a fissure in the soil, followed in quick succession by another, and then another.

I was seeing a mass of snakes, the kind we called striped adders, waking from hibernation. I picked up a nearby stick, and began beating the poor snakes as they emerged. There were probably eight or nine bodies by the time I was through. Perhaps I thought I was ridding the neighborhood of dangerous pests – but I still regret that senseless slaughter.

COES POND

Besides Hendy's and Wooded's as places of aquatic adventure, there was Coes Pond. It took a pretty good hike to get over to Coes from my house, but who had second thoughts about having to hike somewhere? I would take my fishing stuff and head down the hill to Bennett Field. Gates Lane ran parallel to Bennett, and led up past the horse barn to a trail leading through the woods over to Coes, a lake about 20 acres in size.

We knew that Coes, being such a sizable body of water, must harbor some proportionately big fish. In fact, local lore held that there was a massive fish in Coes, who went by the name of Big Joe. I was always keenly aware that every nibble on my line could be Joe. I was prepared to use all the strength I could muster to pull that fish onto the shore. I never did catch him, nor did I ever hear of anyone who managed to hook that monster, but I believed that Joe was in that pond, and I still believe it.

Besides fishing in Coes, I would go swimming there, unless it was polio season. When I say "swimming," I am referring to my paddling around in close proximity to safety. One fateful day, I decided on a whim to swim to the island. This was a small patch of land about 50 yards off shore from the beach area. I made it to about the 40-yard mark when I began to weaken. I went under, but struggled back to the surface. I was achingly aware that no one was aware of my struggles.

I summoned my last bit of energy, took one mighty breast stroke, and felt the blessed presence of the sandy bottom under my toes. I labored up onto the shore and sat down. My next challenge was making it back to the beach area. I rested, plucked up my courage, and slowly made my way back by periodically floating on my back.

I was keenly aware that I had been on the brink of death. I have never felt a greater sense of relief than the moment I could feel that island sand under my feet.

HADWEN PARK

Sometimes, instead of heading down Main Street to Bennett Field, where I played most of my baseball, I would hike down the length of Eureka and turn left past the diner. Taking the next right, I would walk up a steep incline, cross the bridge suspended over the railroad tracks far below, and walk down into Hadwen Park. I mentioned this place earlier, and need to add some details.

While crossing the bridge, looking off to my left I could see the broad expanse of a baseball field, and a broad, dark body of water running along behind right field. In contrast with Bennett Field, every memory of Hadwen Field is tinged with a sense of foreboding and fear.

Why did I go there? Several things drew me there – an invitation to meet kids for a pickup baseball game, basketball games using the hoops set up in the tennis courts and, most often, fishing. I was convinced that the pond held large and hungry fish. When I stood on the shore, I could look off to my left and see that the waters narrowed into a stream that flowed past a smoky factory and a massive coal pile. Every time I fished there, I felt vaguely threatened.

One day, as I was standing on the marshy pond shore, trying to catch what I always imagined would be a large, black fish, I heard a loud grinding sound in the distance behind me. I turned and saw a car crash through the white fence next to the bridge road. It dropped with a grinding clatter onto the railroad tracks below.

I ran towards the scene, along with others in the park, and arrived to see the car in a crumbled heap on the tracks. There were no signs of life. The police arrived quickly. One of them ran up the tracks, aware that this was a busy route, to warn any approaching trains. A photographer snapped pictures. The next morning, my face appeared on the front page of the *Worcester Telegram*, peering out from the crowd. Were there survivors? I don't remember.

I hesitate to recount another aspect of my Hadwen Park experiences, but these memoirs are intended to be comprehensive and accurate. My friends and I led what I can honestly say were safe, protected lives. However, we were somehow at least vaguely aware of possible dangers that lurked "out there." These were personified by two threatening individuals. One of them was known to hang around Hadwen Park. We called him "The Wrestler."

I can see his face now. He was a man, probably in his 40s, who wore glasses. He would try to get young kids to wrestle with him. I never did, but I watched him with a kid once, rolling around on the grass. We knew there was something dangerous and scary about him, but did not know precisely why. I don't recall ever mentioning him to my parents.

The other individual was not associated with Hadwen Park, but scared the heck out of us nonetheless. He lived in our neighborhood, and seemed to be always just wandering around. He had enough ability to work part-time delivering groceries for Morris' Market. Being kids, and living in a time when any mental deficiencies were hidden, and the truly mentally ill were locked away for lack of treatment, we feared *E*, and tried to avoid getting near him. The poor man probably wondered why kids would run away when they saw him.

JOBS

I never felt any pressing need for money except for buying treats like ice cream, candy, or tonic (our name for soda). However, because these were important extras that I craved, I managed to land a couple of jobs.

Looking out from my front yard on Main Street, I could see the broad expanse of Hendy's field. Off to my left, about 500 yards away, stood a large white house flanked by a barn. These were probably built sometime in the 1800s. The property belonged to two elderly women, the Henderson sisters. The locals said that their father had been a ship's captain. The younger of the two often could be seen patrolling her field, shushing away any kid who trespassed. Sometimes, as I headed up the path to the pond, she would advance toward me, waving her broom.

When I was a bit older, probably about ten, I managed to become a Henderson employee rather than an intruder. I had two responsibilities. One was to mow their lawn with an old, balky hand mower. No power grass cutting then. I would also do some weeding in their flower garden.

My other task was more unusual. I was given a mop consisting of a large rag at the end of a wooden handle. I would spill some kerosene from a battered can onto the wooden floors. Then I would rub it in with the mop, while inhaling the fumes. Presumably this was a way to clean and polish the floors.

When I had finished my chores, the older of the two sisters would rummage through her purse and hand me two quarters. Not a bad haul.

My other source of revenue, at least for one summer, was being a paper boy. I signed up to handle the local paper route. This task turned out to be a real pain, which probably explained why I did not last too long.

A truck would drop off a bundle of copies of the evening paper, the *Evening Gazette*, across the street from my house. I would cross the street, cut the rope holding the papers with my trusty Boy Scout knife, and put some of them in my cloth paperboy bag. This was a pouch, open at one end, that I could hang on my shoulder by a broad strap. I walked part of my route, folding each paper so that it would not open when I tossed it on a porch or in front of a door. It took a while to learn exactly where to leave the papers, and I made more than one mistake. I delivered the rest of the papers to the outer fringes of my route by bike.

Every week, I had to go around to each customer and collect money. They were supposed to leave it, in cash, in a small envelope. Of course, they did not always come through. My bookkeeping was irregular at best. This led to some awkward accounting with my handler. This was a man who would pull up in his car and park at the corner of Apricot and Main Streets. He would wait there, as though this were some sort of drug deal. I would approach him and try to coordinate his expectations with what I had collected. In the end, I would depart with some amount of coins as profit.

None of these efforts led to a savings program. However, they did allow me, for example, to stop at the local Texaco station and drop a nickel into the red Coke machine. Out would drop a shapely glass bottle. The Coke ad of the day was "nickel, nickel, nickel, nickel, trickle, trickle, trickle, trickle..." When I had finished my drink, I would place the empty into the wooden box next to the machine so that bottle could be washed and reused.

If it were a hot day, I might walk down to Sal's drugstore and order a "trucker's special." Sal's was not just a pharmacy. It featured a long, marble counter with wrought iron stools, where you could sit and buy ice cream or other cold treats like ice cream sodas or sundaes. The trucker's special, costing 10 cents, was a cone topped by three scoops of ice cream. It took some dexterity to eat that concoction before it began to melt and run down along the cone onto your fingers. It helped if you stayed in the store to get a head start before you went out in the hot sun.

Another common, memorable treat, made possible by having a few coins in my pocket, was heading down to the penny candy store. This was the same establishment that sold fish and chips. Thinking back, I marvel at the patience of the proprietor, waiting behind the counter as I chose carefully among the licorice pipes, the caramel pieces full of nuts, the jelly beans and gum drops, or those large, orange things that looked like foam peanuts.

BOOKS AND MORE

Long, gray afternoons indoors were spent playing games, occasionally listening to the radio, and more often than not, reading. I want to be careful in this memoir to confine my accounts to the period between my birth in 1938 and my time in the seventh grade in the Fall of 1949. When I conjure up my memories of experiences in reading during that time, I am not clear as to their chronology.

I will try to confine my accounts of my early reading life to conform to my most vivid memories. I was an avid reader. I am sure that my love of literature was not sparked by using a school library. I did not attend schools that had a library, or for that matter a gym, a cafeteria, or any other facilities besides the classrooms. However, my neighborhood did have the services of a traveling library that fed and nourished my appetite for books.

Every so often, not far from my house, a light yellow, elongated vehicle shaped somewhat like a large, tapered cylinder would pull up to the curb. It was the bookmobile. The door would open and we filed in, where we would be met with the exciting odor of books.

That sounds somewhat fanciful, but there is a distinct and unique scent to a dense collection of books. In later years, when I worked in the Worcester Public Library during high school, I experienced the gamut of that sensation, from the musty, dusty stacks to the long, colorful rows of books that many patrons had read and returned.

I was fortunate to have been raised in an era when it was assumed that certain books were to be read as a matter of course. I read *Tom Sawyer*, *The Hardy Boys* (many volumes), *Treasure Island, Robinson Crusoe,* stories by Edgar Allen Poe, lots more of Robert Louis Stevenson's works, and Sherlock Holmes. When I look through some of these books now, they seem quite complex for a young reader.

A great deal of reading time was spent in poring over comic books. These could be bought for a dime, and then traded as easily as we traded baseball cards. Every kid I knew had a growing collection of comics – including *Donald Duck, Superman, Plastic Man, The Phantom, Archie, Batman*, and others. My favorite was *Plastic Man*, a hero who could elongate and bend his limbs to reach out and snatch the bad guys with ease.

These immensely popular publications were a handy vehicle for the growing world of advertising. My clearest memories are those on the back covers that featured Charles Atlas. He was a muscular young man, a real person, who promised the reader a way to transform their body from whatever spindly form he assumed you had into a strong, attractive physique. The illustrations pictured a "97-pound weakling" being bullied on the beach. This poor guy would send away for Charles Atlas' training regimen. Following the recommended workouts, he would bulk up, return to the beach, beat up the bully, and regain the admiration of his girlfriend.

Charles' basic workout required the practice of

"dynamic tension." Following his instructions, I would stand in a doorway and push on the frame on either side. This stress on my muscles was supposed to trigger them to grow. The same principle could cause my chest muscles to grow when I squeezed both arms on one side of the doorway.

I certainly did my best to grow bigger with this practice, but I gave up after a while. Perhaps I was too optimistic. Besides, this was an era when attempts at strenuous muscle building were considered almost dangerous. Even if you succeeded, you ran the risk of being "muscle-bound," unable to move freely. That was never my problem.

In addition to the wildly popular comics, I also enjoyed *Classics Illustrated*. This was a series of "comics" that recreated famous works of literature as illustrated stories. There were works like *The Three Musketeers, The Count of Monte Cristo,* and *The Last of the Mohicans.* Apparently, intact copies of some of these, as is the case with the everyday comic books, are now worth hundreds to collectors.

My piles of comics and baseball cards, and those of my friends with whom I traded, are long gone – but stay in the memories of lying in bed, and using a flashlight under the covers, sneaking a look at the latest acquisition.

RADIO AND TV

While we had yet to experience the miracle of television in our homes, I can relate several specific and vivid television memories. The first scene was probably in 1947. I was eleven years old. My father and I had walked down along Main Street all the way to Webster Square. When we arrived at the store where television sets were sold, there was a crowd of men already gathered outside, gazing intently through the store window. They were waiting for the event we had come to see – the heavyweight championship bout between Joe Louis, the champ, and Jersey Joe Walcott, the contender.

I don't remember who won the fight, but I do remember the warm feeling of being a part of a group, a masculine crowd of yelling guys who had let me into their number.

It was not unusual then to catch big televised events by simply heading for the nearest window display. After all, who could afford their own TV? We would eventually get one when I was in high school. It was a box the size of a bureau, full of glowing tubes. It had a screen measuring about 15 inches diagonally.

Before we had the luxury of owning a television set, my sister Rosemary, two years older than me, baby sat for the *M* family. When she went over there, a couple of streets away, I would follow after the adults had left. This was our chance to watch the popular early TV series

I Remember Mama, "Brought to you by Maxwell House Coffee, good to the last drop."

On one such evening, I decided to search the pantry for something to eat. I found a box of cookies and we both dug in. They weren't that tasty, but after all, they were free for the taking. The second batch was even worse than the first. A closer inspection of the box revealed that we had been eating dog biscuits.

The closest my immediate family got to the growing TV culture were the occasional visits to Uncle Walter's house. Walter, my father's older brother, lived a short bus ride away, down near Saint Peter's church. He and my Aunt Lily had three or four offspring with whom we had only periodic contact. However, those Sundays when we would all descend on the relatives were the most sociable times I can remember as a kid.

When we arrived, the front room would be in darkness. Uncle Walter's family would be gathered in front of a television set the size of a kitchen cabinet. The screen was about a foot or so in size, on which some kind of program in black and white would be playing. The fascination lay not in the details of those long forgotten performances, but in the fact that they could be seen, live, on that magical box.

At some point, Lily would go back to the kitchen and put together refreshments for everyone. There were cold cuts, slices of white bread, condiments, cookies, and tonics. I can still smell the mingled odor of mayonnaise, relish, and cigarette smoke. It was an exotic experience.

Uncle Walter, whom we seldom saw, owned a car. One day, my grandmother, my father's mother, heard that my uncle was coming to the house. I heard her announce,

"Walter is coming over in the machine." Gram had grown up in the days before automobiles existed. They remained a newfangled curiosity to her.

I certainly was more familiar with radio than with television. One important part of our family entertainment centered around the large Philco radio in my aunt Anna's room. The faint yellow dial would glow as we sat listening to a host of favorites, some of which would now be banned as being blatantly racist.

We would laugh at the clumsy speech of *Amos and Andy*, two black men played by two white men, or enjoy Mrs. Goldberg's Jewish housewife antics ("I can't come over, I have a leg in the oven.") Then there were the antics of Fibber McGee and Molly, Fred Allen, Groucho Marx, and Jack Benny. For intrigue, we would thrill to *The Lone Ranger, The Green Hornet,* or *The Shadow.* It was strangely reassuring to know that Tonto, that Native American so loyal to the masked man, would help his "kemosabe" and get the bad guys. Then they would ride out of town, heading for the next adventure.

The Shadow would declare, "Who knows what evil lurks in the hearts of men? The Shadow knows." The main character was Lamont Cranston. He had a female "companion" named Margot Lane. We never wondered what that might really mean.

There were also dramatic plays sponsored by Kraft. There would be sound effects, such as doors closing, footsteps, or the sound of gunfire and horses galloping. Our minds would be put to work imagining the scene instead of passively watching. Sitting in the background would be Aunt Anna, who always seemed to enjoy being the hostess to the gathered children, intent on the radio dramatics.

COMMUNICATING

Recounting my experiences with radio and the early days of television reminds me of another piece of popular technology – the telephone. Not everyone owned one back then, but the big, black rotary dial phone had pretty much become a fixture in our home. All rights to these instruments were the exclusive property of the Bell Telephone Company, or "Ma Bell."

If you wanted a phone installed or replaced, you would need to have a technician come to the house to do the job. Outside the home, there were telephones available for public use in many commercial establishments. Other common sites for phone booths were gas stations and busy downtown streets.

In our neighborhood, one could drop into Sal's drugstore and use the phone booth. Just enter the narrow booth, pull the folding door closed, sit on the small stool if you wanted to, drop a dime into the slot, and the live operator would connect you to a number.

The cost of a long-distance call would be calculated by the operator. She (always a she) would let you know the charge, so you could drop in the correct amount in coins. If you put in too much, she would give you change.

This led to the common habit of checking the coin return tray whenever you passed a phone booth. Many a kid came up with a dime or nickel by doing this simple maneuver.

I am not sure if it was a case of saving a little money, or if the service was not always available, but our phones were "party lines." If the phone rang, the initial peal was either single or double. We knew that if it rang twice, the call was for us. If only once, it was for a neighbor. We were warned to never pick up if it were not for us. Of course, I would do just that to listen in on someone else's conversation.

As a Boy Scout, I knew enough to always carry a dime in my pocket so that I could call for help in case of an emergency. Another technique was to dial the operator and tell her you wanted to make a "collect call." She would dial the number and ask whoever answered if they would accept the charges. If they agreed, you could talk. If you wanted to let your mother know that you had arrived somewhere safely, even if she did not accept the charges, the call itself would tell her you were OK.

VISITORS

We were not a sociable family. I cannot say how our behavior in this regard compared to other families in similar circumstances, and I will not attempt a sociological analysis. I can only report that I can count on one hand the times we had individuals or groups enter our house on Main Street. As for myself, I never had a friend "over" to my house, nor did my sister Rosemary.

On a couple of occasions, my mother's brother Tom came to visit from Rhode Island, bringing his wife and three children. I can see them on the far side of the living room, gathered together uneasily. By the time I was about 12, my mother and her brother would not be speaking to each other, and there would be no more visits.

Two other rare visits occurred. My father had a friend, George, who apparently was a fan of horse racing, and was convinced that he had a "system" that helped him win. One day, he appeared at the front door. He was let in for a brief chat. Then there was the time my mother developed a friendship with a woman who lived nearby. Once, this friend *Lorraine* stopped over for a brief visit. Lorraine would die not long after that, during a polio epidemic. I was not aware of my father or mother having any other friends who ever visited us.

However, my Aunt Anna did have several close friends. Anna was a school teacher. Back then, teachers were almost exclusively female. They were discouraged from getting married. Anna and others kept their jobs by remaining single. Anna's teaching career had been marked by one of her disgruntled students firing a pistol at her through the schoolroom window, an act for which he was jailed.

She had three special friends, *Stella*, *Becky*, and a third whose name escapes me. Two were also teachers, while Becky was a unique woman for her time – she had a Ph.D.

The four of them would periodically get together at the house and play cards. That sounds rather uneventful, but those occasions were exciting and even fascinating for my sister Rosemary and me. They would set up a card table in the living room for their game. We sat dressed in our pajamas, watching them through the slats on the staircase. The visitors seemed quite exotic. They wore fancy dresses, jewelry, makeup, and perfume. To add to the glamor of it all, they smoked and drank alcohol!

This was heady stuff. Drinking, smoking, laughing people in our house – who could imagine such a thing? In the mornings after these visits, the faint odor of cigarette smoke and perfume lingered.

* * *

There were two homes where we would sometimes visit relatives. My grandmother Gram, my father's mother, had two maiden sisters who ran a small boarding house on Russell Street in Worcester. They would rent out rooms to gentlemen who would sleep there, but eat elsewhere. At that time, one of the roomers was their brother John. I remember him as a poor fellow with an ulcerated leg due to his diabetes. He kept his leg enclosed in a long, brown wrapping.

The rooming house kitchen featured what would today give a fire inspector nightmares. There was a large, black cast iron stove that probably was designed to burn wood. It had been converted to burn kerosene. Beside the stove was a platform on which stood a large, glass bottle filled with yellow kerosene. The bottle was upside down, so that the kerosene could slowly trickle into the stove as needed. Even as a kid I thought that looked awfully risky.

Out behind the house, my grandaunts had a large vineyard where they grew Concord grapes. Did they make wine? I never knew. Those elderly ladies, whose names I cannot recall, treated us kids kindly. They served us ginger ale and sugar cookies. We would eat in their sunny kitchen and then wander around, admiring the marble fireplaces and what seemed to be many statues and figurines.

Sady, another grandaunt, lived on Cambridge Street, in a three-decker directly across from Sacred Heart Church. As a kid, my father had grown up nearby, and that church had been his parish until he was married. That area of the city, despite my family history, always seemed to be slightly threatening. There was a cluster of large gas tanks nearby that would slowly rise up and down depending on the volume of their contents. These were across the street from a coal yard, where great black mounds of dusty coal waited delivery. Not only that, the neighborhood was bordered by the Blackstone River, a name that always could send a chill down my spine, especially because I was told that it ran through the city underground.

My paternal grandfather Thomas had operated a grocery store just off Cambridge Street. The only other thing I ever learned about my grandfather, who died before I was born, was that he had been a diabetic. My father never mentioned anything about his own father beyond those two facts. I don't know what that meant.

Grandaunt Sady was married to Thomas Hession, another Irishman in the family. He died when I was about eight. His wake was held in the living room of their home. Afterwards, pallbearers carried the casket across Cambridge Street and into the church. Quite a neat arrangement.

Sady suffered from what was called a "palsied" hand. She was not paralyzed, but could not seem to use her right hand for any strenuous task. (I remember rumblings that this condition was not real, but a form of hysteria.) One day, during one of our infrequent visits, my mother had walked up the street to have her hair "done" in a "beauty parlor," leaving me in Sady's care. During the act of washing my hands under the bathroom faucet, Sady turned on the water, which happened to be steaming hot.

My hand not only reddened, but formed a nasty blister. Sady sprinkled the area with baking soda, wrapped it in some type of cloth, and sent me off up the street to report the incident to my mother. I remember my mother's agitation and anger as she escorted me back to Sady, who took quite a tongue lashing. I don't know if that affected the frequency of our visits to Cambridge Street, but I don't remember another one.

VICES

My 1351 Main Street home in Worcester was hardly a scene of indulgence in the more common vices of humanity. In the early 1960s, I was in on a conversation with a few other graduate students about our mothers. One said, to my shock, that when he thought of his mother he pictured "A woman standing, holding a cigarette in one hand and a drink in the other."

That particular characterization certainly did not apply to either of my parents, grandparents, or aunt. Perhaps that is why three incidents remain with me. Two involve my father, He decided, for reasons unknown to me, that he was going to take up smoking. He brought home a pack of cigarettes and matches. I think they were Lucky Strikes (L.S./M.F.T. – "Lucky Strike Means Fine Tobacco.") He placed the pack on top of the refrigerator – the successor to the old ice box. His attempts to smoke easily and gracefully were short-lived. I don't think his experiment lasted beyond that one pack, and my mother's disgusted reaction.

The same scenario played out during his brief sojourn into the world of alcohol. I don't recall if this happened before or after his fling with tobacco. He brought home a bottle of some type of alcoholic drink, placed it atop the same refrigerator, and proclaimed that he would take a drink each time he returned home from work.

The fallout from that plan was the sound of his retching behind a closed bedroom door.

The other incident revealed to me, even at the tender age of nine or ten, that my Aunt Anna also did not have a good grasp of the world of drinking. I had several cousins, sons of Walter, my father's brother, who were considerably older than me – old enough to drink. Two of them made a rare visit to the house one day. Anna must have known they were coming and had bought a bottle of premade Manhattans. She served them on a tray, in rarely used special glasses. As they were about to leave for the drive home, she went back to the kitchen and came back to the living room carrying the tray with refilled glasses. She said, "Here, finish these up before you get in the car." That seemed like a dangerous offer to me.

My own fling with tobacco was the inevitable experimentation with my friends. This happened twice. A few of my Boy Scout friends and I had come across an almost intact, gleaming white cigarette in the gutter down near the barber shop. We devised a method to share this treasure. We gathered a few acorns and headed down the street to the scrubby woods behind the Fish and Chip store. We cut a hollow reed into a short length, emptied the contents of an acorn, bored a hole into the acorn and inserted the reed. We filled the acorn with tobacco, and had ourselves a nice little pipe.

Of course, as Boy Scouts, we always had matches with us. (I had an extensive collection of match book covers.) We lit up and passed the pipe around. No one wanted to admit that we were all getting a bit green around the gills, along with a growing headache. This was not an experiment that we repeated.

However, I later came upon a mother lode of cigarettes. Someone had dropped an opened pack of Kools in the gutter. These were well known as the brand containing menthol, a chemical that helped soothe the smoker's throat and lungs. I took them up to the woods and tried one. I soon had a massive headache, despite the cool sensation. I tossed the pack into the bushes, ending my brief kid's experience with smoking.

HEALTH

In terms of medical care, in many ways we might as well have been living in the 1840s. I was a kid in the perilous pre-vaccination days. I was inoculated against smallpox, but the other communicable diseases, including measles, chicken pox, diphtheria, whooping cough, mumps, German measles, polio, and others had their way with the population, with many children among the victims.

I ended up, as most kids did, suffering bouts of measles, chicken pox, and mumps. My memories of chicken pox include my mother covering me with Vaseline as I stood naked on top of the bathroom toilet seat.

Infections killed then that now can be cured. A dirty scrape would be cleaned and covered with the antiseptic mercurochrome. This is no longer used due to the danger of mercury, its active ingredient. Antibiotics were not generally available to the public until the mid-40s. The first was penicillin. The effectiveness of that miraculous treatment had been amply demonstrated late in the war.

The scourge of tuberculosis had not yet been kept at bay by antibiotic treatment. Those who contracted that disease up to the mid-40s were whisked away to a sanatorium, where they rested in isolation, dependent on time and fresh air to assist in their recovery, if they were fortunate.

Polio was another dreaded disease for which there was no defense. During an outbreak of polio, we were not allowed to go swimming where there were groups of people, like the Y or the Boys Club, or the local ponds. Paralysis and death were a common result of polio. Victims might be saved by enclosing them in a sealed metal tube – the "iron lung" – which would increase and reduce pressure rhythmically, assisting breathing.

I can see a neighboring house around 1944, across the street from my Howland Street house, displaying a large paper notice attached to the front door. I do not recall which specific disease was announced, but we all knew what that notice meant – Do Not Enter. Compulsory quarantining was the sole protection against a host of diseases.

I was especially prone to catching a cold that would turn to bronchitis. Like groceries, medical care was available locally. My mother would call the doctor, who lived a few blocks away. He would make a "house call," carrying his little black bag. He would listen to my chest, take my temperature, accept a cash payment from my mother, and leave.

She would then apply her favorite treatments for my cough. The first was one that I loved. She would give me a spoonful of Cheracol. That would quickly make me feel calm and sleepy. I never knew that it contained codeine, an opioid.

The other treatment was awful. She would rub Musterole on my chest, covering it with a piece of flannel, despite my pleas. That substance is a greasy material made from mustard seeds ("a trusted favorite since 1905"), whose fumes were supposed to loosen my cough. This was her version of the classic "mustard plaster" used for centuries for ailments of the chest. I hated the smell of that awful stuff, but the Cheracol seemed to take away the sting.

The only real health scare I experienced had nothing to do with disease. My uncle Donald, the son of my father's brother Walter, had come home from the war. He was kidding around with me one day, and decided to toss me up in the air. I happened to be chewing on a piece of peanut brittle. I inhaled a peanut, triggering an episode of coughing and shortness of breath. I was taken off to a local doctor, who somehow managed to extricate the offending object, and I was back in action. My mother seemed to be unhappy with Donald.

FOOD

What did we eat and where did we get it? Certainly, my food world did not include eating at restaurants. "Fast food" establishments had not yet entered the scene, and although there were restaurants here and there, I never entered one until my sister Rosemary graduated from the eighth grade. We went "out to eat" for the first time on that occasion. It was an exotic experience, recalled now in no detail except for a warm feeling of opulence.

The above question would not be asked today. Of course, we would go to a supermarket, grab a basket, and choose among thousands of food items. Back then, such establishments did not exist, at least in my world. Our lives were based on neighborhoods. In mine, as I have related earlier, there were three small grocery stores within one block of my Main Street house.

Directly across Eureka Street there was Kaplan's grocery. On the corner of the next block sat Morris' Market. Across the street from Morris' was the E.T. Smith Company, on the corner of Sylvan Street.

These three small markets were the source of our daily rations. My mother preferred to buy certain items from Kaplan's, and others, mainly meat, from Morris' store. She would hand me a list, and off I would go to the latter. I would walk up to the deli counter, overseen by the owner himself, and bravely say, "One pound of your best hamburg." Morris was a large man who always wore a soiled white apron, and had a gruff manner. He would wrap up the meat in paper, tie it with a string, write the price on it with a black crayon, hand it to me, and bark in a gravelly voice, "Vat else?" I would sheepishly admit, "nothing" and back away.

I would head for the cash register, manned by Morris' son-in-law, Paul. He looked just like Pope Pius, but I could never tell him that. Paul would write down the charge for the meat – it was 29 cents per pound – on a small pad where he kept our account. This was a convenience for the shoppers who would be able to take care of the tab when they got paid at work. All transactions were in cash.

Often, when I bought an item like coffee, lard, or sugar, I would bring along our ration books. These contained small coupons which allowed one to buy a certain amount of these precious goods – their scarcity being a result of the war.

Because it took more ration points to buy butter and margarine, my mother would purchase oleo. She gave me the job of making this vegetable oil product look like the real thing. It came as a soft, white solid in a clear bag, Inside, there was a capsule containing an orange dye. I would squeeze that to break it, and then proceed to massage the bag until it resembled butter.

Kaplan's store was a friendlier scene. Abe Kaplan's son Arthur was a friend, so I felt more comfortable there. Once, Arthur had treated me to an exploration of the store basement. We tried to find a tarantula among the bunches of bananas, but to no avail.

The E.T. Smith company remains a somewhat

puzzling place in my memory. It was a tiny shop where the goods were lined up on shelves which were mostly out of the shopper's reach. The procedure there was to hand the grocer a list of needed items. He would walk around, reaching for those items with a grabber on the end of a long, wooden pole. Not a good plan for generating volume business.

This store was where I would bring cans of fat from my mother's cooking. They would buy it and pass it on to the government for use in the military production of glycerine, useful for explosives and lubrication in the war effort.

This small store eventually went out of business. One day, as I was walking by, I noticed that a large blanket was hanging from the ceiling, blocking a view of the interior. I soon learned that a family of gypsies had taken up residence there. I tried hard to catch a glimpse of what I was sure were colorful, exotic people, but I never got a good look. Eventually, they moved on, like good nomads.

* * *

During my days in the fifth and sixth grades at Gates Lane, I developed a comforting routine. We would be released each day at noon, so those of us who had not brought a lunch could go home to eat. By the time I had walked up the hill to 1351 Main Street, my mother had put out on the table an American cheese sandwich on white bread with mayonnaise, a bowl of tomato soup, and a glass of orange tonic. While I ate, I could hear the daily noon news on the radio.

After I ate, my mother would hand me a nickel.

I headed back to school. On the way, I would buy a peppermint patty at Kaplan's for my dessert. I can still taste it.

* * *

My mother was a good cook. That judgement is not meant in any epicurean sense. He spices were salt and pepper, and her choices reflected her Irish roots. Her father had been from Quebec, but her mother (Nana) was of Irish ancestry, so I assume that my mother had been raised on the subsistence diet of meat and potatoes.

She seemed always to be in the kitchen or pantry. I have no memories of anyone else doing any kind of food preparation. My two grandmothers and my Aunt Anna lived with us, but beyond showing up for meals their domain seemed to be limited to the living room, dining room, or their bedrooms. The idea of a grown man like my father cooking would have seemed absurd.

The dinner menu, always served at six, typically consisted of a meat – roast beef, pork or lamb chops accompanied by mint jelly, hamburg, chicken, or steak. There would be potatoes, either mashed or boiled, and a vegetable. This was often a canned vegetable, like peas, or corn (kernel or creamed), beets, carrots, or the dreaded Lima beans. For dessert – there was always dessert – we might have cookies, cake, or maybe Jell-O or Junket. The Jell-O might have fruit cocktail suspended in it. Junket is a kind of flavored custard that is now hard to find in the grocery store. I loved it, as well as my mother's delicious rice pudding, full of raisins.

Dinners for the children were always accompanied by a glass of whole milk, poured out of the glass quart bottles left on our back doorstep by the milkman. There would be sliced white bread and butter. The latter would have been dropped off by the milkman, and the bread left by the bakery deliveryman.

My mother's cakes, especially her white cake with chocolate frosting, were superb. Once, as I was feasting on a large slice of that cake, I told Aunt Anna, "When I grow up, I am going to make one of these and eat the whole thing myself." I can see the curiously sad expression on my aunt's face as she said, softly, "No, no, no you won't." I did not understand this message from adult world until many years later.

Unfortunately, there were times when my mother would succumb to a popular idea about childhood nutrition. One was the practice of "Fletcherizing." This practice had first been popular in the late 19th century. It was promulgated by a food faddist, Horace Fletcher. He taught that each mouthful of food should be chewed 32 times before swallowing, in order to achieve complete digestion. Somehow, by the 1940s, this idea had evolved into requiring 100 chews.

For a mercifully short time, my mother insisted on this routine. I assume that she had to quit this experiment when the meals took too long, and the potatoes cooled off.

However, she did insist, for a much longer period, that we eat everything that was on our plates – the classic "finish your vegetables." My most vivid and painful memories of this are staring at a scoop of vile orange summer squash on my plate. I would manage to get through it by either taking tiny bites, or mixing a dollop of squash with my mashed potatoes. There was often gravy that helped as well. The same scene applied to

Lima beans, those pale, green, unnaturally large blobs, or to turnips.

Our breakfast was usually a meal of dry cereal or oatmeal. My father's mother, Gram, would sit at the end of the Formica dinner table and eat a bowl of Quaker oatmeal. To my horror, she would take a piece of toast, dip it in the oatmeal, and eat it. How could she have tortured a kid like that?

After she ate, Gram would dissolve a couple of small, black tablets in hot water. These were Bell-Ans, a 19th century remedy for indigestion. Only much later would I understand and empathize.

My mother, may she rest in peace, fed us many tasty meals. There were probably multiple factors that formed my adult attitude toward meals – they are something to do out of necessity.

HORSES

The 1940s society in which I grew up utilized horses, just as in prewar days. That changed quickly as the 1940s morphed into the 50s, but in my childhood, horses were part of the daily scene. I am not writing here about race horses or polo ponies. The horses I knew were blue collar hauling horses, the bedraggled looking nags that pulled delivery carts through the streets.

There was the rag man and his horse, dragging an old wooden cart piled with rags. He would stop at the corner of Eureka Street and shout, "Raaags, Raaags." Housewives would come out to the curb and hand over rags that they no longer needed. The rag man would weigh them on a scale hanging down from the back of the cart, and pay a few cents for the goods. The old horse would stand by peacefully, sometimes munching from a canvas food bag suspended below his mouth, waiting to amble on to the next corner.

Sometimes the ice man would show up at the front curb in a white, horse drawn wagon. He would get out, move to the rear, open the gate, and reach in for a big block of ice. Using a crescent shaped hook, he would grab that ice and throw it up onto his shoulder, which was protected by a leather apron. He would go in the back door of the house and place the ice block into the chamber in the top of the ice box. We would hang out near the ice wagon in the summer months, because the ice man would usually chip off a few pieces for us.

How did he know when to stop? He would make a delivery whenever he saw the sign displayed in the front window that said simply, "ICE." That reminds me of another sadly common window sign of that time. It was a large gold star, indicating that a member of that family had been killed in the war.

Down in Webster Square, just as one entered the first intersection, there was a busy blacksmith shop. The front doors were often open, and you might see the blacksmith inside, bent over, shoeing a horse.

My fondest horse-related memories are the times late at night in the snowy winter, when I was lying in my bed. I could hear the approach of a sleigh with its jingling harness gliding along Main Street. After a heavy snow, given the less than efficient snow removal of the time, there was a good surface on which to enjoy a brisk sleigh ride.

DELIVERIES

Earlier, I mentioned milk and bread deliveries. These were frequent events. We had a metal basket with sections to accommodate several glass milk bottles. After the bottles were emptied they would be rinsed and placed in the basket. This would be left on the back porch, along with a note indicating our orders for milk, butter, and eggs. Early in the morning, before I got out of bed, I would hear the milkman rattling that basket as he took the empties and replaced them with full bottles topped with paper caps. Sometimes, before we got to the delivery, a bird might peck at the cap and sometimes succeed at reaching the cream layered on top of the milk. Our milk would be "homogenized" by a vigorous shaking before pouring. If we wanted cream, we could simply decant it.

Breads and pastries were dropped off at the same site by the Cushman bakery man. He would also respond to a paper order form, and leave bread and various delicious pastries.

We also had exciting deliveries by the coal man – at least they always seemed to be a dramatic process to me. The coal truck would pull up, and a man, blackened with coal dust, would get out and head to the back of his truck. He would pull out a long metal chute and haul it along the cement walk paralleling our house.

Opening a small rectangular window in the foundation, he would insert the ladder, which would reach down into the coal bin.

The bin was a large area set off by a low wooden wall from the rest of the cellar. Next to the coal bin sat the squat furnace, swathed in a thick layer of insulating asbestos. A pipe containing a length of steel fashioned into a large screw about five feet long connected the bin with the furnace. The screw, driven by an electric motor, would turn slowly and convey the coal into the furnace where it could be burned, aided by an air blower.

Such a system required "pea coal." These were pieces that were about the size of a large grape. The coal man, after putting the chute in place, would go back to the truck and fill a large canvas bag held in a metal frame. He perched this on his shoulder and carried it back along the house to dump it onto the chute. It would descend with a great, dusty clatter. He would repeat the task until he had filled the order.

The coal system was not perfect. There were times, all too often it seemed, when the coal contained pieces that exceeded that ideal grape size. They would enter the screw mechanism, jamming it. You could hear the poor mechanism groaning with the effort. My father would call for me to help. We would go down the cellar stairs – it could be at three or four o'clock in the morning – and we would go into a well-rehearsed routine of taking apart the screw and removing the offending lump. We might have to re-ignite the flame – a tricky operation. It was a bonding experience, like going to Aubuchon Hardware, or helping him with home repair projects, often bungled.

Other more mundane deliveries were those of the mailman and paper boy. There were two mail deliveries, morning and afternoon. We also received two newspapers daily. These were the *Worcester Telegram* and *Evening Gazette*. How else to learn the news of the day besides the papers, radio broadcasts and the occasional viewing of international news in between the first movie and the main feature at the local theater in Webster Square?

ENTERTAINMENT

There were a few group activities that left a lasting impression on me. I am including going to the movies as one of them, although I always went alone. It seemed that kids just convened there at the Park Theater on Saturday afternoons to form a noisy, enthusiastic, packed house.

I would walk down to Webster Square and head for the small movie theater on Park Avenue. Admission was 25 cents, which got you an introductory B-grade movie, a few minutes of Movietone News, followed by a feature presentation. The News was a special treat because it often included scenes from exotic sites such as London or Paris.

When you entered the lobby of the theater and began to look for a seat, a uniformed usher would accompany you down the aisle, using a flashlight to guide you to an empty spot. The same ushers were kept busy during the screening. They would use those flashlights to illuminate kids engaged in some noisy activity or scuffle that sometimes led to an expulsion of the troublemakers.

Most of the movies were black and white. However, one memorable production was, "The Boy with Green Hair." I found out years later that this was an antiwar movie, but I think much of that message was lost to me at the time.

The movie projectors were rather noisy, which was not a problem for us. However, the film would occasionally jam. As the audience watched helplessly, the film slowly melted and the picture disappeared.

* * *

Going to the movies was great fun, but even better was the rare trip to White City, an "amusement park" in Shrewsbury. This was just over the Worcester line, not far from downtown. It was the sort of place that you would go to on some sort of outing, such as you might have with the Boy Scouts, or your Church.

My few trips to this exciting venue were in a group with a priest from Our Lady of the Angels parish, although I am not sure which one. This was many years before the era when parents would have second thoughts about sending their kid on a jaunt with a cleric.

White City was a magical, busy venue on the shore of Lake Quinsigamond. It was an impressive sight to a kid, with its hundreds of lights strung along a circus type midway. There were white wooden buildings here and there housing a penny arcade, games, and best of all, the Fun House. Once inside the latter you were free to choose whatever activity you had the courage to attempt.

I had three favorites. The first was a gigantic wooden barrel lying on its side. It rotated slowly, so that when you walked into the opening you were immediately forced to keep walking forward, but at an angle. That usually didn't work well enough to keep you upright, so you would be carried up on the surface until you tumbled back down. I am not sure that today's safety precautions would have allowed that degree of battering.

The second was the polished, wooden, wavy slide. It reached to the second story of the building. You had to climb a long flight of stairs, grab a ragged piece of burlap, sit on it, and launch yourself downward. You could get a pretty good burn if you came in contact with that surface on the way down. The exhilarating descent could then be repeated as long as you had the energy.

Then there were the wacky mirrors. If you entered a hallway and walked straight ahead, the floor became slanted, and at one point a sudden blast of air from a hole in the floor gave you a sudden scare (and raised the girls' dresses). You would then come upon several large, curved mirrors that made you appear bloated and misshapen.

The Fun House was everything its name promised. It was filled with screams, laughter and shouts, and only occasional sobs.

Just outside the Fun House there was a large, glass enclosed structure about the size of a telephone booth. Inside sat a life-sized figure dressed as a gypsy. She had a large nose, dark eyes, and a fierce expression on her face, framed by a red turban. She sat there, immobile, until you placed a coin into a slot. She would slowly look up at you, and then her head would move back and forth, scanning some cards. She would indicate her choice with a menacing finger, and her prediction of your future would slide out into a tray on the front of the booth. Then, she would resume her silent wait. Her piercing gaze was enough to scare the daylights out of you.

Milder entertainment was found in the penny arcade. The most interesting feature there, at least to me, was the viewer into which you gazed while turning a handle. You would see a cartoon, created by a series of still images, one after another. This was a "peep show" of the innocent variety.

Or you might try out the machine that, marvelously, would imprint the Lord's prayer onto a penny. There was also the "love tester." Just by grabbing a metal handle and squeezing as hard as you could, the machine would measure your romantic potential. Not a bad deal.

Over by the water was the imposing roller coaster. This offered a terrifying ride at breakneck speed. I tried it once, but never wanted to repeat the experience. It was scary enough to ride the airplanes. These were near the water also. These were model planes suspended on cables. As the assembly rotated, gaining speed as it turned, the planes would rise until you were riding at about a forty-five-degree angle. That was enough of a thrill for me.

* * *

The mother of all spectacular experiences went far beyond the movies and the amusement park. This was the arrival of the Ringling Brothers and Barnum & Bailey Circus. In the late 1940s I was just the right age to savor the excitement of the whole circus spectrum. This extended from the arrival of the animals by train and their parade through downtown, to the setting up of the massive tents with the help of the elephants, and finally, the three-ring show itself.

The circus set up in Beaver Brook Park, a large field about three miles from my home. The workers and animals arrived in a crowded, bustling, colorful array. The large animals like the gorillas and lions and tigers were placed here and there in cages. The tent poles supporting the heavy, white canvas main tent were raised by having elephants haul on the attached ropes.

All this was done under the supervision of workers who were called "roustabouts." Someone had told me that if any of these itinerant laborers got in trouble they would shout, "Hey Rube," and their co-workers would rush to their aid. I kept expecting that this would happen, but I never did hear that cry.

They would also raise a separate tent for the "sideshow." This was an amazing and, in retrospect, a sad collection of unusual human beings on exhibit – people we referred to as "freaks" without a second thought.

When the circus was underway, there was a barker outside the sideshow whose job it was to lure people inside. That was not hard to do, because this show was wildly popular with every age group. There was another show, presumably for adults, that I could not enter as a kid. The barker announced that inside one could see "girls" that were "tall, tan, torrid and terrific." I did, however, get into the show that featured a creature who "walks and talks and crawls on her belly like a reptile." This turned out to be a woman who appeared to be dressed below her waist in some sort of scaly costume – a bit of a disappointment.

Back to the sideshow. This was arranged so that the crowd circulated along the periphery of the tent's cavernous interior, stopping at each human exhibit. I can see each of those clearly. First, there was the sword swallower. He would insert a long blade down his throat as he arched his head backwards. Did he just use a collapsible sword? Oh, no, because he then would insert an illuminated tube so that the audience could see the light shining out through his belly.

The "Fire Eater" did just that. Lighting a mass of what looked like cotton, he would stuff it into his mouth and extinguish the blaze. Then he was able, somehow, to blow out a long stream of fire to the astonishment of everyone.

The "Rubber Man," dressed only in shorts, could twist and knot his limbs in seemingly impossible ways. Next to him was the tattooed man and woman. At the time, the sight of a man, and especially a woman, covered with elaborate decorations was extraordinary. Our only experiences then with tattoos were the navy veterans, who might go so far as to decorate their arms with a small anchor or heart. Today, one can see circus-like coverings almost anywhere.

The "tallest man in the world" stood there in his gigantic cowboy boots. Once, I happened to be close to the stage, so I reached out and touched his boot. His angry voice boomed down at me, telling me to stop. Of course, I stopped immediately.

The most interesting person on display was Freda Pushnik, billed as "The Armless and Legless Wonder." Little Freda had been born without limbs. There she sat with a pencil in her mouth. For a quarter, she would write her name on a card for a keepsake.

Near Freda's platform was a family of midgets. They were perfectly shaped, miniature people, with the parents and several kids, dressed formally, sitting there saying hello with their small midget voices.

Two ladies were next. One was the "Bearded Lady." She was simply a woman with a bushy black beard. The other was the "Fat Lady." She probably weighed about 400 pounds. She sat eating a large wedge of watermelon, with a forlorn expression on her pudgy face.

What did I think of this spectacle? Did I feel sorry for any of these people on exhibit who were transported from city to city, all across the country, to be ogled by thousands? I don't recall any such emotion – just awe at the spectacle.

* * *

The main show under the "Big Top" was an awesome panorama, combining acts going on simultaneously in three adjacent rings under the direction of a "ringmaster." He described the action through the loudspeaker as the jugglers, trapeze artists, high-wire acts, trained horses, and other performers kept up a whirlwind of activity. Colorful and sometimes scary clowns patrolled around the periphery of the rings, eliciting shrieks from the kids lucky enough to be sitting down in front.

Why all the excitement? To a kid in the 1940s, the sights to be seen in the circus were only available, if at all, in books or magazines, or maybe sometimes in the movie theater. When the circus came to town, a new and exotic world could be experienced firsthand. How else could a kid stare a lion or a gorilla in the face, separated only by iron bars, or see someone risk their lives by walking on a high wire with no net under it? And what about those elephants walking slowly in single file from the circus train down along Main Street?

* * *

Entertaining as well were the few times the whole family, minus the grandparents, spent a summer week at

Hampton Beach. We rented a small cottage on one of the short streets that run East to West off the main drag at Hampton, site of the famed casino. I have no idea how we got there because we did not own a car. It was great fun to be all gathered together in that bungalow, just a short walk from the crowded beach. It's difficult to draw a sharp contrast between the Hampton of those days and today. The casino, amazingly, remains almost identical to its attractions of yesteryear – the noisy games at the arcade, the shooting gallery, and the alluring smell of fried dough are all still there.

Each morning, my father and I would get up early and walk to a nearby bakery, where we would buy fresh donuts to bring back to the family. During the day, we would sit on the beach, splash in the water, and try to avoid sunburn. These days were, in my mind, simple, uncomplicated times.

The same can be said of our few trips to Boston on the train. South Station in downtown Worcester was a cavernous, bustling nexus for trains heading out to and arriving from exotic locations like Springfield, and even beyond. In Boston, we especially liked to ride in the Swan Boats. Rosemary and I would run after the pigeons in Boston Common, and never manage to catch one.

DOWNTOWN

World War II ended in 1945, when I was seven years old. Lifestyles would evolve quickly away from the austerity of the war years, but much in the late 40s differed little from prewar days.

There were no malls, no fast food establishments, no big-box retail stores. Even if one were to suddenly appear, there would be too few car owners to keep it in business. Instead, the commercial life of Worcester was in the center of the city, which we all called "downtown."

Beyond food and pharmaceuticals, buying whatever goods one might need required a trip to this bustling mix of stores, featuring prestigious "department" stores – Filene's, Denholm's, Richard Healy's, or Barnard's, as well as specialty shops like Ware Pratt for men's clothes, or Thom McCann's for kid's shoes.

My mother loved to shop, and often took me along. Her idea of shopping was to look at what seemed to me to be pretty much everything in the store before deciding on a purchase. My concept of shopping was to know what you wanted before you got to the store, and then walk in and buy it. That continues to be my approach.

My mother and I would walk across Eureka Street and get the downtown bus in front of Kaplan's grocery store. When we neared our destination, she would let me pull the cord running above the windows along the length of the bus. That would let the bus driver know that we wanted to get off at the next stop.

Not wanting a reluctant kid by her side on her shopping forays, she would offer me a bribe. If I accompanied her with a minimum of complaints, she would take me to Woolworth's. They had a long, marble counter with padded stools. It was a classic "soda fountain." First, I would order a piece of chocolate layer cake. This would be followed by a chocolate ice cream soda. If it were a hot summer day, I might instead get a hot fudge sundae and a lime Rickey, a delicious, cold drink of lime juice and seltzer.

Our forays into the department stores were an introduction to a luxurious environment, at least in my eyes. The goods were displayed in glass-enclosed counters, behind which stood elegant ladies ready to assist. Each floor of the buildings housed different categories of items. To go above the first floor, patrolled by a polished gentleman, the "floorwalker" who would answer all inquiries, we would use the elevator. This was run by a uniformed operator who would open and close the brass door. He would announce the identity of each floor, saying "ladies garments" or "men's clothing," etc.

Less elegant, but equally busy, was the shoe store. I had an experience there, that if repeated today, would be met with horror. After the clerk measured my feet, I would try on a pair of stiff, leather "school" shoes. Did they fit? To find out I would be led to a large machine. I would place my feet into a slot at the base of this machine. The clerk would turn it on. Looking through a screen just below my eyes, I could see the bones in my feet. It was an x-ray machine, a fluoroscope!

What could be a better example of "how times have changed?"

EPILOGUE

As I sit here in my favorite chair, I realize that in a few weeks it will be my 82nd birthday. When I look out the window to my right, I can see a patch of woods across the street. It seems that I started this adventure wandering in woods, and now I have come full circle, still peering into the trees – but with poorer eyesight, and less spring in my legs.

No matter. I can still run across Main Street and climb up that grassy field to Hendy's Pond. The sun will feel warm on my back, and the fish will be biting. I will listen to the chorus of bullfrogs, and hear the cows lowing in the pasture over behind the farmer's place.

And now, I hear my mother calling me home for supper, so I had better get going. She will worry if I am late. My father's probably home by now, sitting down to read the newspaper.

They'll want to know what I've been doing all this time…

Thomas F. Lee, Ph.D. retired after 35 years as a biology professor at a New England College. He is the author of seven nonfiction books and a novel.

Made in the USA
Middletown, DE
20 July 2020

13217363R00106